THE EUROPEAN C

Innovation, policy learni
cohesion in the new kn
economy

C000151482

Graham Room

in collaboration with Jacob Dencik, Nick Gould,
Richard Kamm, Philip Powell, Jan Steyaert,
Richard Vidgen and Adrian Winnett

First published in Great Britain in September 2005 by

The Policy Press
University of Bristol
Fourth Floor
Beacon House
Queen's Road
Bristol BS8 1QU
UK

Tel +44 (0)117 331 4054
Fax +44 (0)117 331 4093
e-mail tpp-info@bristol.ac.uk
www.policypress.org.uk

© Graham Room, Jacob Dencik, Nick Gould, Richard Kamm,
Philip Powell, Jan Steyaert, Richard Vidgen and Adrian Winnett 2005

British Library Cataloguing in Publication Data
A catalogue record for this book is available from the British Library.

Library of Congress Cataloging-in-Publication Data
A catalog record for this book has been requested.

ISBN 1 86134 739 1 paperback

A hardback version of this book is also available

Cover design by Qube Design Associates, Bristol
Printed and bound in Great Britain by MPG Books, Bodmin

Contents

List of figures and tables

Figures

Tables

Preface

This book arises from work undertaken at the University of Bath during 2001-04, as part of the NESIS (New Economy Statistical Information System) project. Our final report, submitted in August 2004, offered a critical appraisal of the various indicator sets which were available to benchmark the new economy. This book builds on that work, setting this appraisal in the larger context of debates about policy benchmarking, governance and globalisation. I am grateful to my co-authors for allowing me to undertake this task, even if the result is one which does not do justice to the full range of work which they undertook within the NESIS project.

NESIS was funded by the European Commission as an Accompanying Measure within the Framework 5 Research Programme. We are grateful to the Commission for permitting the work that we undertook for the NESIS project to be used in this publication.

The NESIS consortium was coordinated by Informer SA (Greece): the other partners were the European Commission's Joint Research Centre, ISTAT (Italy), Statistics Finland, Statistics Netherlands, University Bocconi (Italy) and EU-qualify (Italy). We record our appreciation of this collaboration and in particular the leadership of the consortium by Deo Ramprakash. Other materials from the NESIS project can be found via our website http://www.bath.ac.uk/soc-pol/research/nesis/

The authors are responsible for the material in this book and neither the Commission nor the rest of the NESIS consortium are committed to its argument.

In the course of the NESIS project, a number of external advisors played a significant role in supporting the NESIS work programme and enriching our discussions. Foremost among these were Tony Clayton, Christian de Neef, Clark Eustace and Dario Togati.

Several Research Officers contributed to the NESIS work at Bath and, although they were not part of the authorship of the final report, their contribution should also be acknowledged: Claire Johnstone, Kevin Marsh, Victoria Petrie, Diana Robbins.

Finally, we gratefully acknowledge kind permission from the European Information Technology Observatory (EITO), the International Telecommunications Union (ITU), the Organisation for Economic Co-operation and Development (OECD) and Sage

Publishers to reproduce tables and figures from various of their publications, as indicated at appropriate points in the book.

Graham Room
University of Bath
April 2005

ONE

The new knowledge-based economy

New economy, new society?

The closing decade of the 20th century saw widespread claims of economic and social transformation: centred on the new information technologies, but going way beyond technology in its ramifications. To make sense of this transformation, to evaluate its positive and negative consequences and if possible to steer its development became a central priority of public policy makers. It is with some of these efforts that this book is concerned, with particular reference to the European Union.

Claims that the industrial economy was being overtaken by new economic and social forms were of course nothing new. Nor were the hopes placed in technology, as the means of meeting human needs, reducing the need for toil and creating the conditions for social peace. Alfred Marshall, addressing the Cambridge Reform Club in 1873, posed the question as to whether technical progress would eventually make possible a society where heavy physical toil was eliminated and "every man is a gentleman" (Marshall, 1925). In the 1960s liberal writers such as Kerr and Bell – and, more ambiguously, Galbraith – placed similar hopes in the technological dividend to be enjoyed by the market societies of the West (Kerr, 1964; Galbraith, 1967; Bell, 1974). This would be a post-industrial society, with technical knowledge and information a principal driver of progress and its possession the new basis for social and economic power (Kumar, 1995).

Meanwhile other sociologists debated the transition from Fordism to post-Fordism, as the dominant paradigm of production (Jessop, 1991; Amin, 1994). Since the 1970s, the Fordist paradigm had been beset by dysfunctions between its different levels of organisation: worker resistance to the rigidity of the division of labour; globalisation of economic activity creating problems of national regulation; patterns of consumption which, being more varied, could not be satisfied by mass production. Computer-based technologies would enable the organisational networking and core-periphery reconfiguration that the post-Fordist production paradigm required. The next 'long wave' of development would therefore have the new information technologies at its heart: reshaping markets, spawning new industries and revolutionising the management of space and time.

Within more recent debates, (see, for example, Rubenson and Schuetze, 2000; Castells, 2001; 2004) a number of key elements emerge as the focus of academic theorising: these include:

- the role of the new information technologies as a 'general purpose technology' pervading all areas of production, distribution, consumption and governance;
- the new and more flexible organisational architectures associated with the 'network economy' and their relationship with dynamic growth at the level of the enterprise and the region;
- the accelerating pace of innovation – both technological and organisational – and the consequent restructuring and volatility of social and economic relations;
- the growing importance of knowledge as a factor of production and the implications for investment in human resources and lifelong learning;
- the institutional forms appropriate for ensuring transparent governance, economic flexibility and security under these new conditions.

The debates of the 1990s and the new century have, however, been more than a simple continuation of the earlier discussions, if only because of the changing public context in which they take place. Personal computers are everywhere and through the internet they link everyone – or at least everyone who seems to matter. Fears of general computer chaos, as the year 2000 approached, underlined the centrality of these new technologies to all aspects of everyday life. The proliferation of new internet-based businesses with spiralling stock market valuations dominated the business pages. So did the remarkable period of inflationless economic growth in the USA during the Clinton years, coinciding with the spread of the new technologies, but creating fears in Europe in particular of being left behind in this new economic race. Meanwhile, the international political context had also changed. The demise of the Soviet Union – state-sponsored Fordism – left American high-tech entrepreneurial capitalism as everyone's role model. It had also left no competitors to America's international political hegemony. The *Pax Americana* and the internet defined the technological and the political terrain on which a new sort of global socio-economic order was being created.

The debate about the knowledge-based economy is therefore, perhaps inevitably, a debate also about the process of globalisation. Here two principal positions may be distinguished. On the one hand are writers asserting or assuming that contemporary processes of globalisation – economic but also political and social – are bringing about – or are closely associated with – a new phase of industrial or post-industrial development, towards which most if not all countries are being drawn (Giddens, 1990; Castells, 2001). This is in some degree a reworking of longer-established convergence theory, with a strong dose of neo-liberal ideology, foreseeing the progressive assimilation of national differences of socio-economic setting. Against this are ranged writers for whom these national differences in socio-economic institutions and political settlements remain crucial prisms through which the effects of globalisation are mediated: there are 'varieties of capitalism' and there are good theoretical and empirical grounds for expecting that there will continue to be a variety of trajectories of socio-economic development (see also Esping-Andersen, 1990; Crouch et al, 1999; Brown et al, 2001; Goldthorpe, 2001; Hall and Soskice, 2001; Longstreth, 2005).

Figure 1.1: IT/GDP versus per capita GDP in Western Europe, the US and Japan, 2002

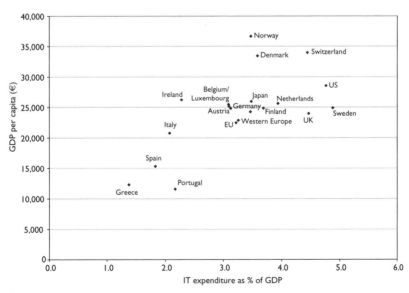

Source: EITO (2004)

In successive chapters of this book, we seek to address these scholarly debates. We also however engage with the debates among policy makers at national and international level: their more pragmatic concerns, hopes and anxieties in regards to the new knowledge-based economy.

The policy debates

The OECD – the club of the richest industrial countries – has been the principal international forum within which policy debates around the new knowledge-based economy have taken place. In recent years the OECD has produced a number of reports which aim to bring together the most up-to-date policy research and promote debate on the alternative paths of socio-economic development that countries are pursuing.

The New Economy: Beyond the Hype (OECD, 2001) was produced as part of an attempt to understand differences in macroeconomic growth performance across the OECD, and as a complement to OECD work on environmentally sustainable development. It appeared just as the 'dot.com bubble' was bursting – hence perhaps the report's title. Nevertheless, its conclusions are self-confident. Something new is indeed taking place in OECD economies, associated with the new information technologies, and making for higher levels of productivity and economic growth. However, investing in ICT per se may achieve little; and a strong ICT production sector is neither necessary nor sufficient for a country to enjoy the benefits of this new economy. ICT seems to facilitate productivity growth only when accompanied by appropriate investment in human skills, organisational change, innovation and entrepreneurship. It is on these interrelated elements, and the policies to support them, that the rest of the report focuses. The concerns that emerge from *Beyond the Hype* are that countries should understand these complementarities as the context of their ICT investments: the new knowledge-based economy will not spring ready-made from the keyboard of a computer.

Beyond the Hype started from the different patterns of economic growth manifest in different OECD countries and it assessed the contribution of ICT and a range of complementary inputs. *OECD Information Technology Outlook* (OECD, 2002f) started from the other end: the ICT industry, the applications and impacts of ICT across economy and society, and policy options as far as ICT is concerned. Some of the report deals with trends in the ICT producing industry: the continuing acceleration of computing power and communication capabilities; new software applications; the globalisation of the ICT

Figure 1.2: ICT investment by asset in OECD countries, 2000

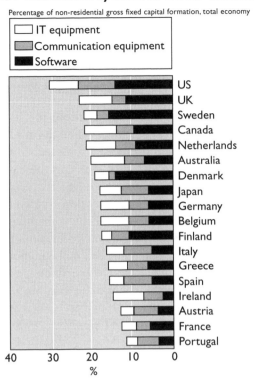

Percentage of non-residential gross fixed capital formation, total economy

Source: OECD (2003a)

sector (its share in international trade and the patterns of cross-border alliances and acquisitions). However, much of it is also concerned with wider applications and impacts and the factors which may drive or inhibit these: building trust in the security of e-commerce; overcoming skill bottlenecks, especially skills relating to software applications in business settings; avoiding a 'digital divide' which leaves some countries, regions, businesses, households and individuals lagging behind.

Finally, *ICT and Economic Growth* (OECD, 2003b), a product of the OECD Directorate for Science, Technology and Industry, returns to the concerns of *Beyond the Hype*. It reassesses the relationship between ICT and business performance and the implications for aggregate productivity growth, in the light of the latest empirical research. In particular, it draws together a range of firm-level studies that explore the interrelations between ICT and other investments, the organisation of work and appropriate workforce and management skills. From these studies emerge a number of insights into the ways that the new knowledge-based economy can best be realised: the use of ICT-enabled networks to integrate value chains and establish close relationships with customers and suppliers; the role of training, enabling workers to be proactive in applying new ICT systems; the importance of the regulatory and competitive environment, in providing the impetus for firms to be radically innovative.

These are reports providing a broad panorama of patterns and trends across the OECD member states and assessing the scope for policy interventions to steer the new economy. There are, in addition, a range of OECD reports concerned principally with statistical indicators of these developments and the technical problems these pose: these will be brought into our discussion in subsequent chapters. Finally, there are OECD materials which deal in greater detail with individual policy arenas: for example, the role of ICT in reshaping the learning environment of schools. Again, these will be left until later chapters.

This international work feeds off, and into, similar efforts at a national level. Given its pioneering role in the new economy, those offered by the United States are of particular significance. Since 2000 the US Department of Commerce has published an annual appraisal of the 'digital economy' (US Department of Commerce, 2000; 2002a; 2003). These have been concerned, first and foremost, with developments in the ICT producing sector, but looking beyond these to applications of ICT across economy and society more generally. The policy concerns expressed in these reports are broadly in line with those already covered in our treatment of OECD publications, albeit with their mood strongly coloured by the changing fortunes of the American economy: bullish in 2000, struggling with the slowdown in 2002, optimism returning in 2003.

Finally, looking beyond the rich world, there has been a growing debate about the consequences of these new technologies for international development. The most obvious forum at which these concerns have been expressed is the World Summit on the Information Society, launched at Geneva in 2003 and due to reconvene in Tunis in 2005. The principal sponsors include the United Nations, the OECD, the EU and the International Telecommunications Union (ITU), but a wide variety of non-governmental organisations and technical groups have also been involved. The central concerns have been the dangers of a global 'digital divide' and the scope for extending to the developing world some of the benefits of the new knowledge economy. Other global initiatives sharing these concerns include the G8 DOT Force initiative (Shade, 2003), the Commonwealth, the high level ICT task force of the UN (see www.unicttaskforce.org), the World Bank, the

Digital Bridges Task Force (see www.gbde.org) and the Global Digital Divide initiative of the World Economic Forum (see www.weforum.org).

Scope of the new knowledge-based economy

What is the new knowledge-based economy? How does it relate to the 'old' economy? Is it the same as the digital economy, the information economy, the intangible economy and the network economy? How does the information society relate to each of the former: and does 'society' here include or complement 'economy'?

Scholars and policy makers have to some extent used these various terms interchangeably: definitions have been left implicit. Within both the OECD and the EU, there are parallel strands of work referring to the information economy, the new economy and the knowledge economy, covering overlapping terrains but with no clear overall guide as to their interrelationships (OECD, 2001; European Commission, 2002d; 2002j; 2003a; 2003h). Some efforts at conceptualisation have been made by national statistical offices, concerned to establish agreement as to the boundaries and content of this 'new economy' if they are then expected to gather relevant statistics. One good example is Statistics Sweden (Statistics Sweden, 2002; 2003; 2004); several other useful contributions are included in IAOS (2002). However, even these efforts have not ventured much further than an eclectic *tour d'horizon*.

Nevertheless, it is important to recognise that the policy and statistical communities have faced major difficulties in conceptualising and measuring the knowledge-based new economy. Different statistical and policy working groups, charged under a variety of remits with reporting on recent economic and social changes, have interpreted the latter through the lenses of their respective remits, but without any clear overall framework. Conceptual diversity is not the only problem. Equally important, the fact that statistical systems are still very much geared to the 'old economy' means that all those who seek not only to conceptualise these developments, but also to measure them, are torn between what existing statistics can reveal and the data that new concepts properly require. Many of the EU and OECD publications mentioned above serve a vital function, in deploying existing statistics for the purpose of illuminating current socio-economic transformations, but severe constraints are imposed by the conceptual underpinnings of those statistics.

What seems clear is that it is unfruitful to conceptualise this new economy by reference to particular sectors (for example the ICT-

Figure 1.3: ICT investment is accompanied by rapid innovation in ICT

ICT as % of non-residential investment, 1998

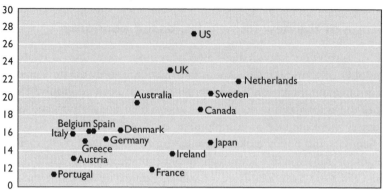

Correlation = 0.59
T-statistic = 2.84

Share of ICT patents in all patents, 1998

Source: OECD (2003b)

producing sector), factors of production ('knowledge workers'), technologies (ICT and maybe other 'general purpose technologies' such as biotechnology and nanotechnology), products (digital), markets (global versus national and local) or organisational architectures (downscoping, outsourcing and delayering), even if these all play their part. Nor is it particularly fruitful to compare nations by means of indicators measuring their capacity or performance, on each of these dimensions taken separately. It is more useful to conceptualise and measure the interrelationships and complementarities among these elements, in enabling trajectories of dynamic transformation: albeit trajectories which may have negative consequences – in terms of stagnation and exclusion – for other actors.

Accordingly, for the purposes of the present study, we treat the knowledge-based new economy as referring to the production, exchange and use of knowledge services involving the innovative application of ICT. It therefore includes not only investment in ICT itself, but also:

- the reshaping of business processes and socio-economic institutions to exploit the new possibilities that ICT offers;
- the human investment in management and workforce that will enable this technological and organisational innovation;
- the use of ICT to manipulate and exploit other general technologies of the modern world;

- the opportunities which ICT affords to develop new organisational architectures, including the 'network economy';
- the interrelationship between the communications revolution which ICT affords and broader processes of globalisation – and indeed the more general reconfiguration of spatial relationships.

Conclusion

It is with reference to these scholarly and policy debates that we now pose five principal questions, around which the argument of this book is organised:

- How are we to conceptualise the modes of dynamic transformation which this allegedly new economy involves?
- What benchmarking indicators will allow us to track these transformations?
- Can these indicators be used to inform public debate and improve their governance?
- How far does this new knowledge-based economy allow alternative paths of development?
- What are the respective places for national, regional and global action to shape these paths?

We pose these questions with particular reference to the experience of the European Union. Chapter 2 examines how the EU has set about addressing the challenges of the knowledge-based economy and the role of policy benchmarking within this strategy. It also however notes some of the ambiguities within this strategy: ambiguities which then play out through the rest of the book.

The EU strategy is born in part of the process of economic and monetary union and is devoted therefore to securing fiscal stability and economic growth. These are the concerns of Chapter 3. In that Chapter, however, we argue the need for understanding the dynamism of the new knowledge-based economy in terms that go beyond conventional mainstream economics: not least, if the EU is to pursue effectively its wish to create a dynamic and innovative economy. To elaborate this understanding is the task of Chapter 4.

Chapters 5, 6 and 7 examine these processes of dynamic transformation in relation to enterprises, human investment and social cohesion, and appraise the benchmarking indicators by means of which these transformations can be tracked. What each of these chapters highlights is that these trajectories of transformation are contingent upon the institutional context and, to this extent, allow of alternative paths of development.

Chapters 8, 9 and 10 draw out the implications of this analysis in three respects. The first of these chapters considers the implications for modelling and measuring the new economy and offers an overall appraisal of the benchmarking indicators which the EU has been employing for its drive towards a knowledge-based economy. Chapter 9 is concerned with the role of benchmarking in relation to governance. The final chapter sets this EU experience within a global context and draws out the implications for the debates on globalisation with which the present chapter began.

TWO

The EU response

Introduction

The European Union has long been preoccupied with the fear of falling ever further behind the economies of the United States and east Asia. During the 1980s the main barrier to European economic development was seen as being the fragmentation of different national markets: the response was the drive to create a Single Market, a project which was in principle at least to be completed by 1992 (Cecchini, 1988). With a single home market, European enterprises would, it was hoped, be able to operate on a scale to match their American and Japanese rivals. During the 1990s economic and monetary union consolidated the project.

During the late 1990s the focus of attention shifted to the new information technologies and their associated economic transformations. The fear now was that the US would run away with the knowledge-based industries of the new economy, while east Asia – China in particular – would capture the manufacturing industries associated with the old economy. This would leave Europe with a bleak future. Moreover, the globalisation of the economy – the result in part of political initiatives, notably the rise of the WTO, and in part of the rapid communications and 24/7 working which the new technologies have enabled – meant that these challenges from North America and Asia would become more and more pressing. Europe had nowhere to hide. Even the notion that China would concentrate on the old economy, and leave the 'triad' of Europe, North America and Japan to divide out the new economy, began to look forlorn (Schaaper, 2004).

Recognising these dangers but also the opportunities, the Lisbon European Summit in March 2000 set a new strategic goal for the Union for the new decade: "to become the most competitive and dynamic knowledge-based economy in the world, capable of sustaining economic growth with more and better jobs and greater social cohesion" (Presidency Conclusions: European Council, 2000b, para 5). This not only asserted the ambition to play a central role in the development of the new knowledge-based industries: it also reaffirmed a long-standing goal of European political economy and – implicitly at least – a critique of the American: to temper the flexibility and insecurity of the market with high quality social protection and an active public policy.

The assumption here – common across the countries of the EU – is that public policy makers can intervene in order to promote the dynamism of the economy, or at least to address its socially negative side effects. There is, admittedly, a contrary view, and one that seeks support from the outstanding performance of the US. This is that interventions by public policy makers are likely only to cripple the creative energies unleashed by the new economy. It would be better to leave these energies to produce new waves of Schumpeterian 'creative destruction': there may be victims of such change, but matters will only be made worse by public intervention: ultimately many more will suffer from those interventions than will benefit. (This view overlooks, however, the important role of US Government contracts – defence in particular – in supporting the development of high-tech innovation: Nelson, 2000).

Be that as it may, the Lisbon Summit established a new approach to policy development, with the aim of promoting a concerted European drive towards the knowledge-based new economy, and encouraging imitation of the best performers (both within the EU and outside). Central to this was the notion of policy benchmarking, using appropriate statistical indicators which would compare national performances, both within the EU and by reference to the USA in particular. This chapter examines this approach to policy benchmarking and initial efforts to apply it to the knowledge-based economy.

Our assessment of the Lisbon process – in particular policy benchmarking – in relation to the knowledge-based economy covers the initial five year period. It therefore broadly coincides with the mid-term review undertaken by the European authorities. This review process started in 2004, with the publication of the so-called Kok Report (European Commission, 2004a). Here is not the place to review and evaluate this report. Suffice to say that the report, while it endorses and reaffirms the broad thrust of the Lisbon strategy, including the Open Method of Coordination, concludes that by and large the strategy has had only limited success. The mid-term review has continued through a series of public documents issuing from the European institutions, which broadly endorse the Kok conclusions, but seek then to relaunch the Lisbon process in a streamlined and more coherent form (European Commission, 2005a; 2005b; 2005e). In the concluding chapters of this book, we return to the Kok agenda, in the light of our own analysis, and we consider how well-grounded are the policy recommendations it offers.

The Lisbon process

The Lisbon strategy for a concerted European drive towards the knowledge-based new economy included three distinctive elements (De la Porte et al, 2001):

- the coordination of a wide range of policy instruments within a framework collectively agreed among the member states;
- the promotion of benchmarking, exchange of good practice and peer review, in the so-called 'open method of coordination';
- the involvement of a wide range of actors in new modes of governance.

A coordinated policy approach

The Lisbon Summit anticipated that a wide range of economic, technological, social and employment policies would be needed in order to achieve its strategic goals. Previous EU Summits had made no less sweeping reference to a wide range of policies: this was the first to set in motion a process by which all these policies would be 'joined up'. Across a broad array of policies, all intended to promote the drive for a socially cohesive knowledge-based economy, a number of central preoccupation are evident, which will provide the focus for the central chapters of the present study.

First, the Lisbon Summit was concerned with the macroeconomic health of the EU. As the Summit noted, the Union was experiencing its best macroeconomic outlook for a generation: the Single Market was a reality, public finances were in good order and the Euro had been introduced. Economic growth and job creation had resumed (European Council, 2000b, para 3). However, this European economy was being transformed by the information revolution, to an extent perhaps as great as the first industrial revolution: the consequences were difficult to understand, let alone predict. Since the Lisbon Summit, the rise of the new economy, seemingly unstoppable, has faltered but then, at least in the United States, has resumed. Meanwhile, in the European heartland, economies stagnate and show little sign of catching up with the US. Macroeconomic growth and stability are in question.

Second, as the Lisbon Summit recognised, the new economy would not emerge from the womb of the old, unless there were further structural reforms at the micro-level, to improve productivity and competitiveness (European Council, 2000b, para 5). This would need to include concerted R&D policies and improved communication infrastructures, which could themselves benefit from the new information and communication technologies. The 2000 Action Plan *eEurope: An Information Society for All* (European Council and European Commission, 2000) therefore made reference to the role of ICTs in developing a faster internet for researchers on the one hand, improving communication and transport infrastructures on the other. What would also be important was to identify and support the organisational architectures that favour dynamic innovation.

Third, the Lisbon Summit looked to a knowledge-based economy which gave a central place to skills and training. Policies for human investment were therefore of central interest. Meanwhile, if new organisational architectures in enterprises are a key to success in the new economy, the same organisational strategies were being tested among education and training institutions. What remained unclear was precisely how human investment policies could drive the new economy and the ways in which education and training systems could best deliver these.

Fourth, the Lisbon Summit affirmed its confidence that the new economy would promote employment and social inclusion: a European trajectory distinct from the liberal insecurity of the American. However, it also recognised that these fruits could not be taken for granted. In the new economy as in the old, the accelerating pace of change, while it opened up new employment opportunities, also rendered precarious traditional patterns of employment and placed a heavy burden on systems of social protection. It also thereby imposed new strains on the European social model, which would have to be reconfigured if it was to play a positive role in the information society. Here again, the delivery of such policies could benefit from the new ICTs: the Action Plan *eEurope: An Information Society for All* (European Council and European Commission, 2000) made reference to the role of ICTs in improving access to public services, including health care.

Benchmarking and the open method of coordination

The Lisbon Summit established a new form of policy coordination among the Member States (European Council, 2000b). The 'open method of coordination' (OMC) involves:

- fixing guidelines for the EU as a whole, combined with specific timetables for achieving the goals which they set in the short, medium and long terms;
- translating these European guidelines into national and regional policies, by setting specific targets and adopting appropriate measures, taking into account national and regional differences;
- establishing, where appropriate, quantitative and qualitative indicators and benchmarks against the best in the world and tailored to the needs of different Member States and sectors, as a means of comparing best practice;
- periodic monitoring, evaluation and peer review, organised as mutual learning processes.

The open method of coordination (OMC) is distinctive in a number of respects. It involves 'soft law' rather than Treaty-based legislation. National responsibility for the policy areas to which the OMC applies is not put in question: subsidiarity is respected: nevertheless, member states commit themselves to collective goals and disciplines. The overall aim is policy coordination, policy learning and performance improvement, so that Europe and its constituent nations can be at the leading edge of global economic performance.

The OMC was applied first to the areas of employment policy and social inclusion. In the employment field, where even before Lisbon the OMC had been pioneered through the Luxembourg employment process, the cycle of annual national reporting has bedded down, and the peer review orchestrated by the Commission has not proved as anodyne as some predicted (Barbier et al, 2001). In the field of social inclusion, the first round of national reports were submitted in 2001 and the second round during summer 2003. Other policy domains where elements of the OMC have been introduced include education (European Commission, 2001g), immigration (European Commission, 2001a) and pensions (European Commission, 2001f). Benchmarking is also proceeding in other policy domains, albeit not couched in terms of the OMC: in respect of competitiveness, for example, championed during the 1990s by the European Round Table of Industrialists and now taken forward by DG Enterprise (European Round Table of Industrialists, 2001). The backcloth for all of these is provided by the Commission's *Structural Performance Indicators,* dealing with broader changes ranging from financial markets, R&D and productivity, through employment and poverty, to environmental indicators such as greenhouse gas emissions and energy efficiency (European Commission, 2000c; 2003e).

The OMC has prompted a variety of wide-ranging academic and policy debates. Our focus will be on the benchmarking processes and indicators that are being used in relation to the new knowledge-based economy. We will, in addition, consider some of the implications of these for processes for EU governance.

New modes of governance

The Lisbon Summit moved beyond the traditional demarcation of national and Community competence and responsibility. Areas of national competence were now brought together in a common and cooperative endeavour: a process that involved 'soft' policy making rather than 'hard' legal process, but which was not self-evidently inconsequential. The potential implications for EU governance have attracted widespread comment: on the one hand the new relations which the OMC establishes between national governments, the EU institutions and civil society, on the other the struggles between social and economic ministries and directorate generals of the Commission for control of the OMC process (De la Porte and Pochet, 2002, ch 1; Borras and Jacobsson, 2004). These questions will however be left in the background as far as the present study is concerned.

The open method of coordination (OMC) is distinctive also in the role which Lisbon gave to a wide range of actors beyond national governments. This seems to have been driven in part by fears about the democratic deficit of EU policy making: a deficit which the OMC threatens to exacerbate, separate as it is from formal scrutiny by the Parliament. It also, however, betrays recognition that in many of the policy fields with which the OMC deals, there is no strong commitment to a common European destiny, but rather a diversity of national policy preoccupations, and that even at the national level, policy goals are sharply contested. Policy coordination must therefore, it is argued, reach out to embrace a wide range of actors and secure their involvement in the process of policy reform (Lebessis and Paterson, 2001).

In considering what benchmarking indicators may be appropriate for monitoring the development of the new economy, it will be necessary to consider their utility for policy actors. However, under the Lisbon process these policy actors go far beyond the EU institutions and their statistical services, to include all those who are involved in shaping or debating public policies to steer the new economy across the EU. This includes enterprises working at European level and making use of EU indicators, in order to plan their own activities and to engage in discussion of EU competition policy. It also, indeed, includes citizens more generally, in so far as they engage actively in debate on the direction of EU policies concerned with the new economy and are in need of transparent, clearly understandable indicators, in order to take a meaningful part in such debate. To these issues of EU governance we return in later chapters.

First efforts at benchmarking the knowledge-based economy

The EU has developed a number of indicator sets for monitoring and benchmarking the development of the new knowledge-based economy. These include three in particular: the eEurope action plans and indicators for 2002 and 2005 (European Council, 2000a; European Commission, 2001b; European Commission, 2002e); the European Innovation Scoreboard (EIS) (European Commission, 2002b); the science and technology indicators of the European Research Area (ERA) (European Commission, 2002j). These indicators are being used in regular publications, reporting the progress of the EU member states, judged against each other but also by reference to the USA and Japan. This progress is presented along with an assessment of existing policies and the identification of policy guidelines for the future, to support the move towards a knowledge-based new economy. These reports parallel similar exercises that are proceeding under the auspices of the OECD (OECD, 2001; OECD, 2002d; OECD, 2003a).

The eEurope action plan was an early initiative in pursuit of the Lisbon goals. The initial plan, *eEurope: An Information Society for All* (European Council and European Commission, 2000) covered the period until 2002 and included a series of action points for benchmarking progress in relation to e-Europe. The statistical indicators for this benchmarking were the concern of a Council document in November 2000 (European Council, 2000a) and a further Commission document *eEurope: Impact and Priorities* in March 2001 (European Commission, 2001b). An updated plan for e-Europe 2005, with a revised set of benchmarking indicators, was published in 2002 (European Commission, 2002e). The indicators focus on the levels of connection to the internet by consumers and business and the degree to which e-commerce, e-government, e-health and e-education have developed (Table 2.1).

The science and technology indicators are supposed to capture research capacity and activity levels in different member states (Table 2.2). They refer for example to R&D expenditure (both public and

Table 2.1: eEurope 2005 benchmarking indicators

A: *Citizens' access to and use of the internet*

A.1 Percentage of households/individuals having access to the internet at home

A.2 Percentage of individuals regularly using the internet

A.3 Percentage of households with access to the internet broken down by device for accessing via digital TV, mobile device (include all forms of mobile access; handheld computer, mobile phone, identifying 3G (UMTS) separately when available)

A.4 No. of individuals with access to the internet broken down by place of access (home, workplace, place of education, internet café, PIAP, etc)

A.5 No. of individuals using the internet for specific purposes (broken down by purposes: sending-receiving emails, finding information about goods and services, reading/downloading online newspapers, playing/downloading games and music, internet banking)

A.6 Percentage of households connected in Objective 1 regions

B: *Enterprises' access to and use of the internet*

B.1 Share of total no. of persons employed using computers connected to the internet, in their normal routine

B.2 Percentage of enterprises having access to the internet

B.3 Percentage of enterprises having a web site/homepage

B.4 Percentage of enterprises using intranet

B.5 Percentage of enterprises using extranet

B.6 Share of total no. of persons employed regularly working part of their time away from enterprise premises and accessing the enterprise's IT systems from there

C: *Internet access costs*

C.1 Costs of internet access broken down by different frequency of use: 20, 30, 40 hrs/week, unmetered rates

C.2 Identification of cheapest access in each Member State in addition to overall basket

D: *e-government*

D.1 No. of basic public services fully available online

D.2 No. of available basic public on-line services with integrated digital back-office processes

D.3 Percentage of individuals using the internet for interacting with public authorities broken down by purpose (purposes: obtaining information, obtaining forms, returning filled in forms)

D.4 Percentage of enterprises using the internet for interacting with public authorities broken down by purpose (purposes: obtaining information, obtaining forms, returning filled in forms, full electronic case handling)

D.5 Public procurement processes that are fully carried out online (electronically integrated) in % (of value) of overall public procurement

E: *e-learning*

E.1 Total bandwidth divided by the number of users/PCs in place of education

E.2 Percentage of universities offering on-line facilities to their students (e.g. information about passed exams, marks obtained in exams)

E.3 Percentage of non-teaching computers sharing the bandwidth

Table 2.1: contd.../

E.4 Percentage of universities/other places of educating offering courses via internet
E.5 Percentage of individuals having used the internet related to training and educational purposes
E.6 Percentage of enterprises using e-learning applications for training and education of persons employed

F: e-health

F.1 Percentage of population using internet to seek health information whether or not for themselves or others. Health information to include injury, disease and nutrition
F.2 Percentage of general practitioners using electronic patient records (easily included in existing general practitioners survey)
F.3 Percentage of prescriptions transmitted electronically between general practitioners and pharmacies

G: Buying and selling over the internet

G.1 Percentage of enterprises' total turnover from e-commerce
G.2 No. of individuals having ordered/bought goods or services for private use over the internet in the last 3 months
G.3 No. of enterprises having received orders via the internet
G.4 No. of enterprises having received on-line payments for internet sales

H: e-business readiness

H.1 Average e-business readiness index value (composite indicator)

I: Internet-users' experience and usage regarding ICT-security

I.1 Percentage of individuals with internet access having encountered security problems
I.2 Percentage of enterprises with internet access having encountered security problems
I.3 Percentage of individuals having used digital signature within the last 3 months
I.4 Percentage of enterprises using authentication (e.g. digital signature) in relations with customers
I.5 Percentage of individuals not having access to the internet at home due to privacy or security concerns
I.6 Percentage of individuals/enterprises that have installed security devices on their PCs

J: Broadband penetration

J.1 Percentage of enterprises with broadband access
J.2 Percentage of households with broadband access
J.3 Percentage of public administrations with broadband access
J.4 Difference between availability and take-up of high-speed internet access
J.5 Broken down by type of access

Source: European Commission (2002e)

Table 2.2: EU science and technology 2002 benchmarking indicators

Percentage of GDP spent on R&D
Government Budget allocated to R&D
Industry-financed R&D as a percentage of industrial output
SME share of publicly funded R&D executed by the business sector
Volume of venture capital investment in early stages (seed and start-up)
Number of researchers per thousand labour force
New PhDs per thousand population aged 25 to 34
Number of scientific publications and number of highly cited papers per capita
Number of patents at the EPO per million population
Number of patents at the US Patent and Trademark Office per million population
World market share of exports of high tech products
Technology balance of payments receipts as a percentage of GDP
Labour productivity – GDP per hour worked
Value added of high tech and medium high tech industries
Employment in high tech and medium high tech Industries
Value added of knowledge intensive services
Employment in knowledge intensive services

Source: European Commission (2002j)

private), the human resources devoted to research and technological development (such as the numbers of science graduates) and the volume of venture capital investment in the early stages of innovation. They also refer to the impact of this research activity, for example in terms of the number of patents registered and the weight of high-tech industries within the national economy concerned. The European Innovation Scoreboard covers much of the same ground (Table 2.3). It also includes a number of additional indicators of innovation, including innovation activities by small and medium-sized enterprises (SMEs), which are particularly important as sources of new employment but which, as we shall see in Chapter 5, can be limited in their capacity to generate and absorb innovation in technology and processes.

Taken individually, each of these domains and indicator sets is of some interest. Nevertheless, as suggested at the end of the previous chapter, what may be needed are indicators which capture, at the micro-level, the intersections and interrelationships among the various elements of the new economy – ICT investment, human skills, organisational change and entrepreneurship – rather than their simple summation. To this extent, the main EU indicator sets look insufficient. To appraise them – and then to go beyond them – is a principal task of this book. This is however no merely technical task. In appraising the Lisbon indicators of the knowledge-based economy, we will be obliged to re-examine the purposes of the Lisbon process as such, and the ambiguity which lies at its heart. It is with this ambiguity that we conclude this chapter.

Table 2.3: European innovation scoreboard indicators

Human resources
S&E graduates (% of 20-29 years age class)
Population with tertiary education (% of 25-64 years age class)
Participation in lifelong learning (% of 25-64 years age class)
Employment in medium-high and high-tech manufacturing (% of total workforce)
Employment in high-tech services (% of total workforce)

Knowledge creation
Public R&D expenditures (GERD – BERD) (% of GDP)
Business expenditures on R&D (BERD) (% of GDP)
EPO high-tech patent applications (per million population)
USPTO high-tech patent applications (per million population)
EPO patent applications (per million population)
USPTO patents granted (per million population)

Transmission and application of knowledge
SMEs innovating in-house (% of manufacturing SMEs and % of services SMEs)
SMEs involved in innovation cooperation (% of manuf. SMEs and % of services
 SMEs)
Innovation expenditures (% of all turnover in manufacturing and % of all turnover
 in services)
Innovation finance, output and markets
Share of high-tech venture capital investment
Share of early stage venture capital in GDP
SMEs sales of 'new to market' products (% of all turnover in manufacturing SMEs
 and % of all turnover in services SMEs)
SME sales of 'new to the firm but not new to the market' products (% of all
 turnover in manufacturing SMEs and % of all turnover in services SMEs)
Internet access/use
ICT expenditures (% of GDP)
Share of manufacturing value-added in high-tech sectors
Volatility-rates of SMEs (% of manufacturing SMEs and % of services SMEs)

Source: European Commission (2003h)

The Lisbon ambiguity

The Lisbon process contains a basic ambiguity. It is in part the offspring of the Maastricht process of monetary union and the Luxembourg employment strategy. Both involved closer coordination of national economic and employment strategies, with member states reporting their performance within a clear and rule-based system, using quantitative indicators. The Lisbon process extended this approach to a broader range of policy areas, in particular those important for the attainment of a competitive and dynamic but socially inclusive knowledge-based economy. This extension was driven in part by the recognition that these other policy areas were significant for the attainment of economic and employment goals: they would therefore need similar top-down disciplines to encourage their convergence. Benchmarking is intended to provide these disciplines and secure policy coordination (De la Porte et al, 2001; Room, 2005).

At the same time, however, Lisbon recognised that in order to develop a knowledge-based economy, the member states of the EU would need to pool best practice and accelerate the transfer of technological and organisational know-how from the best performers to the rest of the Community. Benchmarking for purposes of policy learning and innovation is therefore another element of the Lisbon agenda (European Commission, 2003c). Here, however, benchmarking serves not as a tool of collective discipline, more as a means of coordinating intelligence about different national experiences and enriching national debates. This would seem to require more of a bottom–up logic, allowing political and economic actors on the ground to drive the process of comparison and policy learning, depending on their specific needs and interests. This does not necessarily sit easily with the top-down logic of policy coordination (De la Porte et al, 2001, pp 131-2; for a not dissimilar discussion of alternative models of benchmarking, see Arrowsmith et al, 2004).

As we shall see, this ambiguity in the Lisbon process is no mere untidiness in the debates at the Summit; it also reflects competing policy agendas within national and EU authorities. It is, arguably, because of the failure to address this ambiguity that the Lisbon process has proved to some extent a disappointment, as judged for example by the Kok report (European Commission, 2004c) and the debates it set in motion during 2005. More than this, however, the ambiguity we have identified finds echoes within competing academic paradigms for conceptualising and measuring the new economy. To these we now turn.

THREE

Growth and stability

Policy concerns: the macroeconomy

The US economy enjoyed sustained growth through the 1990s and this, although interrupted during 2001/2 thereafter made some recovery. This was the more remarkable, when set against the performance of Japan and the Eurozone, both becalmed. This was also the period when it seemed that a new economy might be developing, based around the new information technologies. Here also the US was the leader, Japan and the EU the laggards. The implication seemed clear: the new information technologies were driving economic growth, and at an accelerated tempo.

To disentangle the various elements involved in this process, and to measure their respective contributions to economic growth, became a key challenge for national policy makers, seeking to establish where and how to offer support. Should they concentrate on providing fiscal stability and sound macroeconomic management? Or would they need also to intervene to ensure adequate stocks of human capital, an appropriate infrastructure supporting innovation and incentives to entrepreneurship? Questions such as these are at the heart of the major studies of the new economy emanating from the OECD and the US Department of Commerce, as discussed in our opening chapter. The conclusions are fairly clear: fiscal stability and institutions fostering competitive markets are essential and without these, action on other fronts is unlikely to bear fruit.

The stability or instability of the new economy has also been a major concern in public debate. The sustained growth of the US economy suggested that the new economy might provide greater stability of development than did the old; the rise and fall of the 'dot-coms' around the turn of the century suggested the contrary (US Department of Commerce, 2002a, ch 2). Nevertheless, as economies recovered, a modest degree of confidence returned (US Department of Commerce, 2003, ch 1).

Meanwhile, the European Union was forging economic and monetary union, with strict rules of fiscal discipline, as laid down in the Stability and Growth Pact. If the new economy had novel characteristics, in terms of growth and stability, this might prove to be of major significance for economic and monetary union. It would be essential to monitor the development of the new economy, and to secure whatever degree of national policy convergence was necessary, in order to support the stability and growth objectives of EMU. However, the macroeconomic growth performance across the EU has, as already noted, been markedly uneven and in many ways disappointing. It is unclear how far this is due to structural or cyclical factors, and the latter have in any case been modified by the operation of the stability and growth pact. As the EU expands, the greater structural diversity across member economies is another potential source of increased instability.

Partly in response to these policy concerns, the growth and stability of the new economy has attracted significant attention from the mainstream economics profession. It is with their efforts to model and measure these elements, and with the indicators that policy makers might then use to monitor the new economy, that this chapter is concerned.

Growth and productivity in the new economy[1]

For mainstream economists, the first challenge was to measure the new patterns of economic growth and to identify the weight of different factors that might account for them. Neoclassical economics has a long-established toolkit for undertaking such an analysis. It depends upon being able to represent an economy in terms of an overall production function, which relates different inputs to the overall level of output. It also depends upon a number of fundamental – and rather restrictive – assumptions as to how the contributions of different inputs can be measured, by reference to their shares in income (Solow, 1957).

Those who have adopted this approach have found that growth has been stimulated first by the sharp price decline of ICT inputs (notably semiconductors), in line with Moore's Law, and subsequently by the impact of ICT on technical progress (MFP: 'multi-factor productivity' growth) (Jorgensen, 2001; 2003a; 2003b). They attribute percentage point contributions from ICT to growth rates. This can be done directly for ICT investment contributions and, by inference from time trends, for the contribution of ICT to multifactor productivity growth. These findings seem fairly robust, having been repeated by a variety of highly respected authorities (for example, by the OECD Growth Project:

Figure 3.1: Pick-up in MFP growth and increase in ICT use

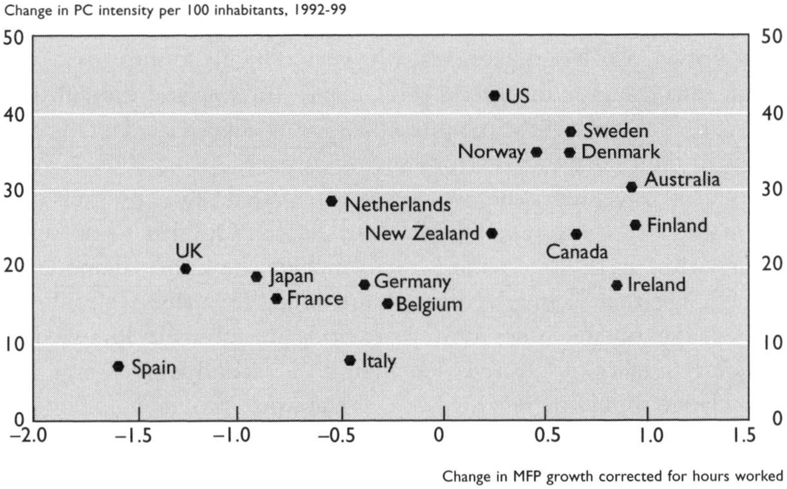

Change in PC intensity per 100 inhabitants, 1992-99

```
50                                                                    50

            • US
40                                                                    40
                                        • Sweden
                          Norway •   • Denmark
30                                        • Australia                 30
                    • Netherlands
          UK       New Zealand •            •   • Finland
20                                      Canada                        20
          •     • Japan   • Germany
                • France   • Belgium            • Ireland
10                                                                    10
      • Spain        • Italy

0                                                                      0
 -2.0    -1.5    -1.0    -0.5     0     0.5     1.0     1.5
```

Change in MFP growth corrected for hours worked

Source: OECD (2001)

OECD, 2001; and, for the Eurozone, ECB, 2003). Individual countries have also conducted similar exercises.

Nevertheless, to repeat, this whole approach depends upon the basic assumptions underlying Solow's position. Some of these relate to problems of aggregation across the economy as a whole. These may in principle be less serious when we look at individual industrial sectors. This has been one of the lines of analysis developed in the *Digital Economy* reports produced by the US Department of Commerce: these bring together industry-level growth and productivity data, so as to identify the contribution to performance due to ICT intensity (US Department of Commerce, 2002a, ch 4; 2003, chs 4-5). What this clearly shows is that ICT-intensive sectors have far out-performed less intensive sectors as far as productivity growth is concerned and that this is true across both manufacturing and services. These ICT intensive sectors have also contributed disproportionately to downward pressure on inflation, in the US at least.

Nevertheless, this approach is subject to a number of qualifications, of particular significance for the new economy. First, with ICT products improving very rapidly, quality changes need to be taken into account, lest the growth in output to which ICT inputs contribute are over-estimated. Various approaches to 'hedonic' measurement have been attempted, involving quality adjustment when estimating the growth of ICT inputs. Without these corrections, the amount of growth in output that is attributed to technical progress is substantially over-estimated (Konijn et al, 2002).

Second, although 'knowledge' presumably plays a key role in the new knowledge-based economy, it is very difficult to measure as an input into the growth process (Hill, 2004). (It is no less difficult for enterprises to know how to capture their knowledge-related intangible assets in their corporate balance sheets: Eustace, 2004a; 2004b.) Two particular conceptual issues will need to be settled before progress can be made with measurement (Winnett, 2004c). One has to do with boundaries: on the one hand how to include the informal and tacit knowledge that is involved alongside more formalised bodies of knowledge, on the other how to exclude the obsolete knowledge which is subject to 'creative destruction'. A second issue is how far knowledge should be regarded as a capital stock, producing a flow of income, and how far as part of the general technology of the economy.

Stability of the new economy[2]

If the first challenge for mainstream economics was to measure and account for the new patterns of economic growth, the second is to assess the stability or instability of the new economy. Within mainstream economic writing, 'stability' is commonly treated as 'convergence towards equilibrium', should the existing economic configuration be subject to shocks. There may be stability within some zones but not within others. From this perspective, there are several possible ways in which the development of the new economy could affect its stability:

- Faster rates of information exchange may make for greater transparency of price and quality and greater 'completeness' of markets, and hence their more rapid adjustment: this could in turn reduce instability.
- In the 'old economy', inventories acted as 'buffers', cushioning the impact of sudden changes in demand. The new information technologies enable tighter management of inventories and 'just-in-time' delivery: this reduces the costs to businesses, but the removal of this buffer may also serve as a possible source of endogenous instability.
- The new information technologies have led to major changes in the financial sector, with scope for more rapid activity but also for runaway 'bubbles': this can however lead to destabilising consequences for the 'real' economy.

- As the new economy develops, it may generate oscillations of greater amplitude; and the zones within which such oscillations tend to dampen down may become more restricted in size. In either case, the new economy could generate instability.

Specific indicators for tracking stability might be defined by reference to changes in share volatility in industrial sectors which are more or less involved in new information technologies. More indirect indicators could refer to differences and changes in frequency of price adjustment, across sectors and over time. Some aspects may be amenable to linking data sets for inventories and for enterprise ICT-intensity.

Nevertheless, to model these various instabilities is very sensitive to the assumptions that are made: and to apply them to empirical data, for the purpose of developing robust indicators, is almost impossible, except on very restrictive assumptions. These are, moreover, challenges which only the most dedicated of economists would even consider attempting (for further discussion, see Winnett, 2004b). This does not, however, mean that they are of no consequence for those interested in the more general functioning of the new economy, whether for purposes of research or policy intervention. Even without empirical testing, the sets of questions laid out above in relation to stability and instability are valuable points of reference for any consideration of system dynamics.

Conclusion

The neoclassical approach to growth accounting and stability that underpins the foregoing discussion depends on a number of rather restrictive assumptions. Here is not the place to explore these in any depth: nevertheless, it is important to notice two of their principal features.

First, neoclassical growth accounting involves measuring the contributions of the various factors of production by reference to their share of income. As we have seen, care must be taken over measurement of these factors: hedonics may have a role to play. We have also seen that it is important to include the full range of inputs: in the 'knowledge economy' it is likely to be particularly important to take account of the intangible inputs associated with knowledge. However, even assuming that these problems can be addressed, neoclassical growth accounting makes the additional assumption that the shares of income received by the various factors of production correspond to their marginal products; and this in turn assumes that there are constant returns to scale (Barro and Martin, 2004; Winnett, 2004a). Against this, it is generally recognised that the new economy is characterised by strongly increasing returns to scale, which play a key part in its dynamic development.

Second, mainstream neoclassical economics generally assumes that the closer that real world markets approximate to perfect competition, with rapid price adjustment, the more stable they will be. However, the real world of the new economy looks significantly different and, as we move away from these mainstream neoclassical perspectives, various other forms of instability come under review (Togati, 2004). Thus, for example, if the spread of ICT leads to the rapid development of new organisational architectures, old architectures could be undermined and instability increased, in face of sudden waves of predatory behaviour. Organisational changes and consequences of this sort are the concern of Chapter 5 and, indeed, in the context of human investment, Chapter 6.

Equally, within a Marxist perspective, the price system is really about sorting out the class distribution of income, not the allocation of scarce resources: this raises questions about the impact of innovation through new technologies on these distributional relationships. Likewise, the very rapid price adjustments that the new economy enables may erode conventional norms of fairness and create a situation of Durkheimian *anomie*: if these spread to the labour market or to the consumer markets dealing with the basic necessities of life, there could be serious consequences for social cohesion. Some of these issues will be at the centre of attention in Chapter 7.

This suggests that what is now needed is to explore more systematically the dynamic interactions between innovation in the new economy and the restructuring of social, economic and political relationships. This is the task of the next chapter.

FOUR

Dynamics and innovation

Introduction

The Lisbon Summit recognised that in order to develop a knowledge-based economy, the member states of the EU would need to accelerate the pace of innovation. This would require structural reform but it could also be promoted by pooling best practice and by transferring technological and organisational know-how from the leading international performers. Benchmarking for purposes of policy learning and innovation is therefore at the heart of the Lisbon agenda.

However, innovation performance has been markedly uneven across the EU member states, and even more so at regional level (which will be shaped in part by the national innovation system within which it is embedded: see below and European Commission, 2002b; 2003c). These questions have become yet more pressing with EU enlargement. Several studies have already identified wide discrepancies in the transition economies' likely capacity for, and responsiveness to, knowledge-based innovation (Piech, 2003; EITO 2004, pp 72-90).

One of our concerns is to identify indicators that policy makers can use to steer and shape these dynamic processes: indicators which may enable the sort of benchmarking for policy learning that Lisbon advocates. Indicators may not be sufficient for such policy learning but they are arguably necessary. We search in particular for indicators which might serve to identify points of leverage – triggers and catalysts – which will send a country or sector along a golden trajectory of socio-economic development (by whomsoever this is defined) or at least steer it away from stagnation and decline.

The risks and opportunities posed by technological advances in the ICT sector arise at least as much from the global as from the national or European economy. As enterprises and other actors develop inventive responses to these technological advances, they draw upon practices and resources internationally, through high tech trade and recruitment of IT specialists in a global market. The indicators which we seek for purposes of benchmarking and policy learning must therefore make reference to national, European and international levels of development.

Mainstream economics does not cope well with the processes of dynamic innovation and cumulative change that would appear to characterise the new knowledge-based economy. The first task of this chapter is therefore to develop a better understanding of the linkages between innovation and macroeconomic processes. This will draw on a wider array of disciplinary traditions, which we draw together in eclectic fashion.

The economic analysis of dynamic change

The previous chapter considered how the growth and stability of the new economy have been addressed from within the mainstream neoclassical paradigm. We noted that the neoclassical paradigm is centrally concerned with the conditions for equilibrium: here in contrast we mobilise a variety of additional strands of economic analysis, more obviously geared to understanding processes of dynamic change.

Dynamism as learning

Much of neoclassical economics assumes that knowledge is freely and globally available: what needs explaining is why not all countries and enterprises are at the frontier of global best-technology practice. National, sub-national and regional economies are arrayed at various points behind this frontier: their position depends on their ability to keep up with the global innovation frontier as it advances, to assimilate innovation from the global economy and to develop innovations which themselves shift this frontier. Some economies may be global innovators, developing innovations from scratch, whereas others may pick up on technologies only at later stages of the innovation process.

Against this, approaches which stress the role of learning-by-doing see knowledge as advancing primarily through its embodiment in innovations, both technological and organisational, which then confer competitive advantage (Kaldor, 1957; Arrow, 1962). What needs explaining is why countries and enterprises which do not get a head start in this virtuous circle should *ever* catch up with – or even overtake – the early leaders, to become the new global innovators.

Both of these processes – the more rapid diffusion of global best-technology practice and processes of learning-by-doing – are emphasised in the literature on the new economy. The former is at the heart of discussions of knowledge management, with enterprises and governments scanning the globe for best practice, new opportunities and impending threats. This is learning-by-scanning. Learning-by-doing raises questions as to the capacity of organisations to adapt to, and exploit, new technologies and production processes, in order to gain competitive advantage. However, their separate treatment within the economics literature may reflect the quest for tractability in terms of modelling, rather than any assumption that only one of them is operative.

Dynamism as endogenous growth

The rise of the new economy has prompted the development of a neo-Schumpeterian growth theory (Aghion and Howitt, 1998 provide a comprehensive and, even now, near-classic account). This recognises that processes of technological progress are shaped by the dynamics of capitalist economies, and that a theory of long-run economic growth must explain why and how technology changes over time. In other words, the technology parameter needs to be an endogenous variable in the model: a crucial weakness in early neoclassical work on long-term economic growth (Solow, 1956; Swan, 1956). One approach pays particular attention to the processes of learning-by-doing already discussed, but also therefore to the role of human capital in achieving sustained economic growth (Uzawa, 1965; Lucas, 1988). A second approach emphasises the role of research activities and hence of the national and international innovation systems: again, human capital has a key role to play, in enabling people to innovate, and to adapt and diffuse those innovations (Nelson and Phelps, 1966). The endogenous growth literature also considers how technological change can increase the demand for skills and cause a rise in inequality, with potentially serious implications for social cohesion (Aghion and Howitt, 1998; Acemoglu, 2001).

The neo-Schumpeterian approach makes far more room for socio-political institutional factors than do most economic models. This is a direct consequence of the endogenising of the innovation process. It quite specifically draws on the institutional matrix as an ingredient in the explanation of variations in growth performance across countries and over time. From the neo-Schumpeterian perspective, institutions can inhibit or enhance the creation, diffusion and impacts of innovation (Jones, 2002, ch 7). For example, the openness of economies to flows of tangible and intangible inputs and the ability of economies to avoid wasteful diversion of resources into sustaining poorly functioning institutions are regarded as crucial factors in explaining comparative growth performance.

Of particular interest for efforts to conceptualise the new economy is the closely related work on General Purpose Technologies (GPTs), which attempts to model and explain long Schumpeterian waves. These technologies differ from other technological innovation in the range of their applicability. GPTs are technologies that can be productively applied to a wide range of sectors, triggering a long wave of continued innovative activity (Helpman and Trajtenberg, 1994). However, David (1990) and Lipsey and Bekar (1995) argue that such GPTs require significant economic and social restructuring and adjustment, and the process of implementation may not be smooth. The implications of GPTs for policy makers are correspondingly more far-reaching than other innovative activity. These perspectives underpin attempts to conceptualise the new economy in terms of 'techno-economic paradigms', for example by Wolters (2003a), with corresponding 'step changes' in the socio-economic system. It is important to recognise the long-term dynamic framework in which these perspectives are set, notwithstanding some criticism that they do not deal sufficiently with short-run dynamics.

Dynamism as external increasing returns: regional agglomeration

The analysis of geographical agglomeration has a long history within economics, albeit one that has been somewhat neglected by contemporary neoclassical writers. Early work by Alfred Marshall (1920) pointed to the benefits that enterprises working in the same industry can derive from such agglomeration, in terms of the presence of a specialised labour force, subcontractors and know-how. This socio-economic homogeneity may also foster the development of social capital and trust. These benefits may then be sufficient to outweigh the negative effects of such concentration: more intense local competition among similar enterprises and physical distance from lucrative markets. If these benefits are sufficiently strong, they set in motion processes of geographical concentration which may become self-reinforcing, while regions which fall behind may be at a growing disadvantage (Krugman, 1991). These external increasing returns may then be coupled with, and reinforced by, processes of learning-by-doing of the sort rehearsed above, on a district-wide basis (Beccheti et al, 2003).

The implications for regional agglomeration in the new economy are not entirely clear. On the one hand, new economy enterprises, being knowledge-based, benefit from the specialist know-how – especially the tacit knowledge – that is brought together in geographical agglomerations of this sort. At the same time, the revolution in communications, which the new economy facilitates, makes it easier for enterprises located in such agglomerations to deliver services remotely, reducing some of the disadvantages of spatial concentration. On the other hand, this improved communication also makes spatial proximity less crucial for rapid communication and the exchange of this specialist know-how (Harris, 1998).

Dynamism as external increasing returns: the network economy

External increasing returns of this sort are not peculiar to geographical agglomerations, they apply to networks more generally. Metcalfe's Law affirms that the value of a network to its members is proportional to the square of its nodes (Metcalfe, 1995). In so far as the new economy permits the development of networks on a much grander and more rapid scale than before, it confers with unprecedented force the external increasing returns which Metcalfe promises.

Networks offer external increasing returns to their members in four main ways (Kelly, 1997; 1999; see also OECD, 2003b, for a discussion of these network effects in relation to ICT diffusion). First, they define common standards for those involved in the network, thereby eliminating the costs of diversity. Second, they provide producers with a 'captive market' for their new inventions – or at least, a market which has already bought into the network's standards and will therefore favour inventions that respect those standards.[1] Third, in attracting new members, they enlarge the ordered universe to which the network gives access. Fourth, they set the rules for admission of non-members and put non-members at a growing disadvantage in the struggle for power and resources.

It is evident from this that the network economy has a very real power dimension. The establishment of a network involves the definition of standards, the capture of loyalty, the exclusion of competitors. The dynamic of the new economy, with its unrivalled scope for developing such networks, is as much one of hegemonic lock-in as of technological advance, especially where this is underpinned by strong legal protection of intellectual property rights (OECD, 2001, para III.2). This has led some to argue that the defence of networks – and of the standards and brands they embody – may become a more central objective of organisational behaviour than continuing innovation (Table 4.1). Others argue that it is precisely by continually extending the range of innovations, that the network offers to its members, that this defence is best undertaken (Kelly, 1997, para 8).[2]

Table 4.1: Proportion of enterprises with innovation activity making use of methods (other than patents) to protect inventions or innovations, by sector, EU, 1998-2000 (%)

	Industry	Services
Formal methods		
Registration of design patterns	15	12
Trademarks	20	2
Copyright	4	11
Strategic methods		
Secrecy	27	28
Complexity of design	17	21
Lead-time advantage on competitors	34	39

Source: European Commission (2004e)

Dynamism as creative destruction

As well as inspiring the new approaches to growth theory described above, Schumpeter is also a point of reference for analysing the behaviour of individual agents within the new economy. Evolutionary economics examines the behaviour of economic agents under conditions of uncertainty and continuous change, taking into account the experience, competencies and routines within the organisation and the larger institutional context in which it is embedded, including the national and international innovation systems (to be discussed later).

As we have seen, neoclassical economics is centrally concerned with the conditions for equilibrium. With profit maximisation the common goal, it is then assumed that firms converge in their organisational structures and behaviour. This hardly captures the dynamic nature of capitalist economies. To some extent endogenous growth theory has attempted to deal with this problem. However, this still takes the firm's choice sets as well-defined and obvious to the firm in question. Any persisting differences between firms, whether in technology or organisation, can arise only from ultimate differences in initial conditions. Given the same conditions, all firms will do the same thing (Nelson, 2000, p 107). However, this inadequately reflects the complexity of the choices that firms have to make in relation to organisation and strategy, and their bounded rationality.

The evolutionary economics literature asks us instead to look more closely at the determinants of the behaviour of individual economic agents. In particular, the emphasis here is on the nature of organisations and how firms behave in an environment of continuous unpredictable change. To ascertain how behaviour is shaped within an evolutionary environment, a more holistic analysis of the interactions between individual economic agents and the context in which they operate is required (Simon, 1957; Nelson and Winter, 1982; March, 1994). In an evolutionary environment a firm needs constantly to adapt to change and take account of new risks and opportunities. The way it does so depends on the experiences, competences and routines pervasive within in given industry. From a Schumpeterian or evolutionary perspective, convergence towards some common form is neither necessary nor likely: differences in strategy and organisational structure would persist, albeit with the emergence of a range of typical or modal forms. (These will be shaped in part by the national innovation system within which they are embedded: discussed later and see Granovetter, 1985.)

Some of the drivers of change within the new economy, to which these economic agents must address themselves, have been outlined in the preceding discussion. Some of them capture with particular ferocity Schumpeter's vision of the 'creative destruction' that characterises a modern economy. The network economy, with its external increasing returns, reinforced by the effects of Moore's law, involves rapidly falling prices of existing products and services, destroying competitors, and the lock-in of users to the next generation of lucrative innovations. On the other hand, the very power of these established networks means that challenges, should they develop, will take the form not of seeking to imitate and undercut existing technologies – something unlikely to be worthwhile – but of technological (and maybe organisational) innovations that are on a quite different terrain. Many will fail, but those that do not may be able to establish new networks of their own, which can suddenly and with little warning outflank prevailing patterns of new economy domination (Kelly, 1997, paras 3, 9).

Taking together the notion of technological regime and institutional embeddedness, a complex evolutionary perspective begins to emerge. This characterises technology not as a force that applies uni-directionally to organisational structure, but which is shaped by generic processes of path dependence and the national innovation system. This helps to explain not only the success stories of firms whose organisational structure and strategy lead to continuing innovation, but also the firms that become stuck and fail. 'Lock-in' occurs when firms compromise their options for development by concentrating only on past or current routines and strategies which have been successful. This suggests that from an evolutionary perspective the firms with the best chances of survival are those which have generated diversified, multiple bases for learning and competency development (Dosi and Malerba, 1996, p 7).

The sociological analysis of dynamic change

Sociological models of organisational learning and innovation

The new economy has accelerated the diffusion of new technologies. The sociological literature that addresses these challenges highlights two interrelated themes: first, the crucial importance of continuous organisational learning; second, the need to address these challenges across the organisation as a whole, rather than limiting them to a central core of managers.

This literature builds critically out of a longer sociological tradition of theorisation of the relationship between organisational structure and behaviour. In Weber's theory of bureaucracy, learning was strongly associated with traditional notions of professionalisation, where stratification separated the educated and qualified 'thinkers' and 'deciders' from the 'doers'. Learning was seen as taking place through qualifying education and any 'topping up' was undertaken at the managerial levels of an organisation (Gerth and Mills, 1948, ch 8). In later 'scientific' views of organisations, associated with Taylorism and Fordism, the emphasis was on the acquisition of technical skills for task efficiency. Individuals were trained to perform a segment of the production process within a highly standardised system. In reaction against this Taylorist image of the organisation as a machine, sociological writers such as Revans (1980) developed the metaphor of the organisation as a system, one which through learning seeks to adapt to the changing demands created by its environment. Continuous change has been a theme of sociologists and futurologists such as Daniel Bell and Alvin Toffler, and it has emerged in the work of theorists of strategic management such as Charles Handy (1989), who challenged managers to accept that change had become a continuous reality, rather than being an occasional interruption to periods of stability.

This systemic approach is also evident in the ideas of Argyris and Schon (1996), who differentiate between learning which is pragmatic and oriented to short-term fixes for immediate problems, and learning which is reflective, questions the underpinning assumptions guiding any modus operandi and is oriented to long term solutions. Senge's (1990) work on the characteristics of the learning organisation similarly stresses 'systems thinking' as a core discipline in developing learning organisations. More recently still, Wenger (1998) has emphasised the social and informal aspects of learning through 'communities of practice': temporary alliances of practitioners seeking collective solutions to practical problems.

Also consistent with these approaches is the work of Rogers (2003), who has developed a model of innovation through organisational learning. Agenda-setting takes place when a general organisational problem, such as a gap between expectations and performance, is identified that may require organisational reform. At the matching stage a problem arising from this agenda is matched with an appropriate innovation drawn from inside or outside the organisation. Redesigning/restructuring involves the mutual adaptation of this innovation and the organisation's structure. Finally, as the innovation is incorporated into regular activity, it becomes routinised.

Sociological models of diffusion

Rogers (1996) also introduced the S-curve for the diffusion of innovations, as well as a typology of population groups in relation to their uptake of new technology (innovators, early adaptors, late adaptors, late majority, laggards) (Figure 4.1).

The focus is on how innovations spread through a given population (households, organisations, etc), once these innovations become available. This is the 'market phase' of innovation. Before this, each innovation has gone through a phase of development and growth (with time ranging from a couple of days to several decades), involving basic and applied research, product development and market research. Development does not however stop with market introduction. The first items sold of a certain innovation can differ substantially from

Figure 4.1: Rogers' (1996) model of diffusion of innovations

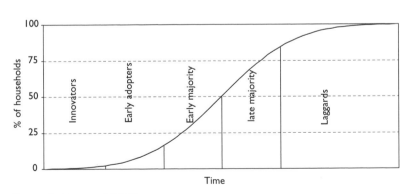

Source: de Haan et al (2003)

later items. As products appear to be catching on in the market, development gets a new boost and incremental changes are made to improve the product or service.

S-curves of this sort have been widely applied. Thus, for example, Industry Canada applies this approach to the spread of e-commerce (Figure 4.2). The S-curve is not fixed, but may be subject to specific policy interventions: investment in knowledge institutions and human capital may increase a country's readiness for the new technology, moving the whole S-curve upwards; such investment may also increase the intensity with which the new technology is used, making the S-curve steeper. Nevertheless, the S-curve is no more than an empirical generalisation and can be both over-simplistic and misleading, depending for example on whether reference is being made to discrete individual innovations, groups of associated innovations and upgrades, or the overall societal-level transition to the new economy.

Science and creativity

There is a long-standing debate as to the respective roles of basic and applied research in the generation of innovations. Already in our discussion of endogenous growth theory, we saw that some neo-Schumpeterian approaches (Nelson and Phelps, 1966) give pre-eminence to basic research activities; others to learning-by-doing (Uzawa, 1965; Lucas, 1988).

Figure 4.2: Maturity of electronic commerce markets and need for indicators

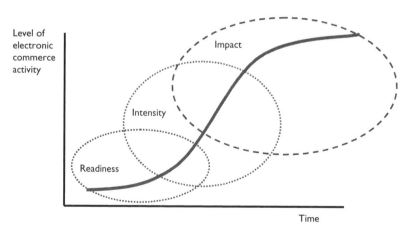

Source: OECD (1999)

During the last half century the major paradigm of science and technology policy in most of the Western world has, arguably, seen basic research as the pacemaker of technological progress (Bush, 1945; Stokes, 1997, pp 3-4). This assumes a linear model of science and technology, and a clear distinction between basic and applied science. Labelled the RDD-paradigm (Glaser et al, 1983), it argues a flow of activity from Research to Development to Diffusion. It follows that it is essential for any national science and technology policy to invest in basic research. Consistent with this was the ambition of the Lisbon Summit to increase the level of R&D expenditure across the EU to 3% of GDP by 2010. Much of the analysis of European competitiveness by the European institutions is also in this vein (see for example European Commission, 2004b, ch 2).

The linear model has, however, come under increasing scrutiny. Through the later part of the 20th century, countries such as Japan could apparently maintain a strong economy without significant investments in their basic research, thereby questioning the predictive nature of the RDD-paradigm. For the critics, innovation depended less on basic research generating new knowledge, more on the creative resources and institutions supporting the application of these new ideas.

One strand of literature has been concerned with the skills of practical creativity with which the workforce is endowed. Florida (2002), for example, is concerned with those in the labour force who use creativity as their critical skill: artists, product designers, etc. His analysis of the 'creative class' in Europe (Florida and Tinagli, 2004) ranks the Netherlands, Belgium, Finland and Sweden as outperforming not only all of the other European countries, but the United States as well. A key proposition of Florida's analysis is that economy follows talent, and not the other way around (see also Room, 2002): for any region or city or country investment in such talent is therefore crucial.

A second strand has been concerned with 'national innovation systems'. Nelson's research (Nelson, 2000), comparing national innovation systems, is persuasive in showing that routines and competencies within firms are influenced by their interactions with key stakeholders in the national innovation system. Despite the globalising tendencies of the new economy, these national institutions create country-specific contexts which influence the path-dependency or trajectory of individual firms and actors and the 'logic' of innovation (OECD, 2001, para III.5; European Commission, 2003a; see also Wolters, 2003b). Among the principal constitutive elements of such systems are four in particular:

- the stocks of human capital which are available;
- the array of knowledge institutions (institutes, knowledge management systems);
- the transaction technology of the economy (the transparency of markets and the enormously greater speed and accuracy of communication);
- stocks of social capital and the readiness of social and economic actors to trust the institutions of the new economy.

This argument, that country-specific institutional contexts shape the specific trajectories which enterprises and countries follow, notwithstanding the pressures of globalisation, extends beyond 'national innovation systems' to labour and welfare regimes, as elements of the socio-political settlements within which socio-economic change unfolds. We have already addressed this argument in terms of the 'varieties of capitalism' debate in Chapter 1 (see also Esping-Andersen, 1990; Crouch et al, 1999; Brown et al, 2001; Goldthorpe, 2001; Hall and Soskice, 2001; Longstreth, 2005). In so far as we take account of these perspectives, our models of dynamic change will make the pattern of transformation contingent upon the specific institutional settings within which innovation takes place.

Conceptualising the new economy

As suggested in Chapter 1, the knowledge-based new economy can be taken as referring to the production, exchange and use of knowledge services involving the innovative application of ICT. It therefore also includes the reshaping of business processes and socio-economic institutions to exploit the new possibilities that ICT offers; the human investment in management and workforce that will enable this technological and organisational innovation; the use of ICT to manipulate and exploit other general technologies of the modern world; the opportunities which ICT affords to develop new organisational architectures; the interrelationships between the communications revolution which ICT affords and processes of globalisation. It is, moreover, the *dynamic intersections and interrelationships* among these various elements of the new economy that are of central interest.

The preceding two sections have highlighted a variety of insights into the dynamics of the new economy that are offered by recent economic and sociological literatures and that any conceptual model would need to recognise:

- Processes of 'learning-by-scanning' and 'learning-by-doing' in 'learning organisations';
- Strong interactions between technological innovation and the restructuring of organisational and institutional relationships;
- Processes of endogenous innovation, with a central place for socio-political institutions in the creation, diffusion and impacts of innovation;
- Increasing returns which lead to diverse trajectories of cumulative innovation, diffusion, hegemonic domination and creative destruction;
- Economic agents as developing their activities under conditions of uncertainty and continuous change, in an 'evolutionary' struggle;
- 'Step changes' in the socio-economic system, involving quantitative and qualitative transformation.

Our conceptual framework (Figure 4.3) considers the *context for innovation* and the various *stages of innovation*. The final section of the chapter then examines the scope for policy intervention: in particular, the implications for policy benchmarking of the sort with which the Lisbon process is concerned.

Figure 4.3: Conceptual model of innovation

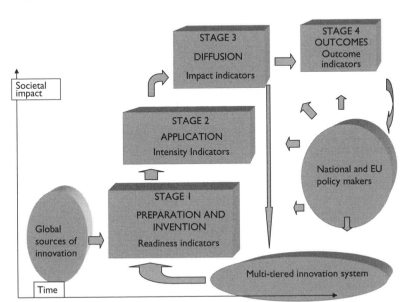

The context for innovation and transformation

Global sources of innovation

The innovation processes of the new knowledge-based economy generate opportunities and risks across a global terrain. These processes include new waves of technological innovation in ICT, but also business processes and organisational architectures that exploit ICT in new ways.

These spurs to innovation arise not within a neutral, apolitical landscape, but within specific political economies, linked to contemporary processes of capitalist development and globalisation. Some economies are global innovators, developing innovations from scratch, whereas others may pick up on technologies only at later stages of the innovation process. The relative positions of different national and regional economies depend upon their ability to keep up with the global innovation frontier as it advances, to assimilate innovation from the global economy and to develop innovations which themselves shift this frontier. The international division of labour is therefore significant in creating and absorbing innovation.[3]

Multi-tiered innovation systems

It does not necessarily follow that national and regional authorities (such as the EU institutions) are therefore powerless: on the contrary, the more that the world becomes a single market place, the more significant that national and regional action to provide supportive regimes for enterprise and development may become (Room, 2002). In particular, the characteristics of national innovation systems will shape the direction and ease of innovation, producing different national performances, which are to this extent path-dependent. Nevertheless, it is important to avoid focusing overly on national systems, as though these were self-contained, neglecting the European and international dimensions on the one hand, the sub-national or regional levels on the other (Cooke, 2004). It is also important to avoid implying that this multitiered innovation system is more 'systematic' than it is: each of its components is being transformed through processes of technological change and socio-economic struggle, and the 'system' is therefore to some extent no more than the untidy outcome of these diverse transformations.

Stages of innovation

Taking into account the various literatures reviewed already in this chapter, we distinguish four stages to the process of innovation.

Stage 1: Preparation and invention

Enterprises, public services and other organisations are exposed to the opportunities and risks presented by new waves of innovation in technology and organisation. The same, indeed, is true of households. These actors scan and plan. They take stock of their own capacities and resources, but also those that are available to them through the national, European and international innovation systems. They devise inventive responses in the light of available leading edge practice, the identification of which may be helped by benchmarking market leaders. The capacity for so doing depends, however, on the extent to which they have refashioned themselves as 'learning organisations', deploying communities of practical creativity.

Stage 2: Application

Having taken stock of the advancing frontier of innovation, organisations selectively embody and apply these in their practices, through a process of learning-by-doing. Households also seek to cope with these new opportunities and risks, investing in their human capital and applying the new technologies in their various life projects. Each of these actors is riding successive waves of change: trying to avoid falling victim to its creative destruction, aiming instead to exploit its potentialities by a process of continuous innovation and transformation. The result can be trajectories of cumulative strengthening and weakening of actors' positions. New technologies and organisational strategies may also, however, offer opportunities for actors to escape, leapfrogging the trajectories in which they have hitherto been locked.

Stage 3: Diffusion

Processes of innovation at the micro-level can have pervasive effects at the macro-level, transforming the whole socio-economic system, especially where increasing returns are pronounced. This can then reshape the national innovation system and the terms on which actors cope with each subsequent impulse. Diffusion can also involve domination and predatory destruction, with those who drive the innovation process setting the terms on which others can henceforth participate in the new economy.

Stage 4: Outcomes

The outcomes of these processes of innovation and transformation are points of reference for the major policy preoccupations which surround the new economy, including its stability, the implications for productivity and competitiveness, the requirements in terms of human resources and the consequences for social cohesion. Policy interventions to address these outcomes may then require attention to any or all of the preceding stages in the innovation process.

It would be wrong to imagine that the movement through these four stages is a simple process of technological competition, in which those inventions that are most fit for purpose will necessarily triumph. The four stages involve a variety of technological and organisational innovations, each of which refashions social, economic and political relationships, with a number of institutional, political, economic and technological factors influencing which of these innovations win out. The analytical challenge, of course, is to pay more than lip service to these complexities, even if they can be modelled only with great difficulty.

There may be parallel streams of innovation, not necessarily synchronised over time. Just as there may be feedbacks among the stages of innovation, these streams may irrigate each other, directly by stimulating new component or product combinations, or more diffusely and intangibly, by stimulating new inventions. Moreover, although we divide the process of innovation and transformation into four stages, it is important to recognise their interconnections, and the conditions under which one develops into the next. Thus, for example, the scanning and preparation of Stage 1 may generate a range of inventions, only some of which are taken up and applied at Stage 2. Similarly, only a few of the innovations and transformations of Stage 2 may enjoy widespread diffusion at Stage 3, with their producers enjoying increasing returns on their investment, locking users into their product standards and seeing the 'creative destruction' of their rivals. To understand the conditions under which these transitions occur is of the greatest importance for policy makers, as they consider how they can support and steer this process.

Furthermore, the temporal and spatial distribution of the four stages between countries may be significant for national prosperity. Thus, for example, those Stage 1 and 2 innovations and transformations which go on to achieve high rates of diffusion are commonly located within the agglomerations of knowledge resource and market power of the leading economies. It is in these same agglomerations that the Stage 3 diffusion of a given technology is likely to occur first.[4]

Conclusion

This chapter set out to understand the processes of dynamic change that appear to characterise the new knowledge-based economy. We have sought to develop an eclectic conceptual model of innovation and transformation, distinguishing four stages in the process of innovation. These four stages are useful for analytical purposes: they also, however, suggest different elements in the innovation process that may need to be benchmarked and different points at which policy makers might intervene.

It is clear that in modelling and benchmarking these processes of dynamic change, it is not enough to focus on technology alone. We need organisation as well as technology in our concept of innovation: institutions as well as markets in our economic models. Our next chapter will take this as its principal focus, examining the relationship between innovation and organisational transformation in the new economy.

Our discussion has implications for selection of the indicators that policy makers might use to steer and shape these dynamic processes: indicators which may enable the sort of benchmarking for policy learning that Lisbon advocates. It will, for a start, be useful for subsequent chapters, if we adopt a taxonomy of indicators which can be readily embedded within our conceptual framework. As Figure 4.3 shows, we propose to use a taxonomy of *readiness, intensity, impact* and *outcome* indicators, with different categories of indicators being assigned to different stages of the innovation process. This particular taxonomy builds on Canadian work undertaken within the framework of OECD discussions (OECD, 1999), where it is embedded within a particular conceptual model of the development of e-commerce (see Figure 4.2 above). Armed with such a taxonomy, we can draw out certain further sets of implications for the sorts of dynamic benchmarking indicators that policy makers would seem to need.

In Chapter 2 we reviewed some of the indicators that are commonly used by official bodies for monitoring the development of the new knowledge-based economy. Particularly common are indicators which deal with what we might describe as readiness for innovation: the science base of different countries, the proportion of science graduates, the degree of take-up of ICT technologies, etc. These are not without value. There are also some indicators that capture the spread across the relevant population (households, enterprises, school, etc) of a particular technological innovation, tracking how this penetration varies between countries and over time. This is relevant to the measurement of the diffusion stage of innovation: it may also be of value in judging the 'readiness' of different industries, sectors or countries for new rounds of innovation.

Nevertheless, our conceptual model suggests that many of the most commonly used indicators of the new economy are insufficiently dynamic. It is important to have indicators of the 'leading edge' of invention and application, capturing the way that successive waves of innovation can reinforce the position of those first able to ride them. Rather than dealing with the diffusion of discrete technologies and innovations, these indicators will be concerned with the way in which enterprises (or industries or households or public services or maybe whole nations) are able to capitalise on one wave of innovation in order better to exploit the next wave, thereby remaining at the forefront of successive waves of change. Only by understanding this leading

Figure 4.4: Proportion of enterprises with innovation activity that considered that their innovation activity had a high impact on specified effects, EU, 1998-2000 (%)

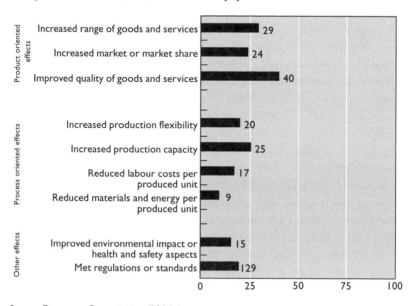

Source: European Commission (2004e)

edge will it be possible to draw lessons for those who are lagging behind and enable them to share in developing – not just imitating – good practice. There are already some indicators of this sort, aiming to capture the intensity of innovation in different national economies. The European Innovation Scoreboard includes indicators of the proportion of enterprises that are involved in product and process innovation (either in-house or in cooperation with others) and the proportion of innovative enterprises that are able thereby to reinforce their position, in terms of increased market share or reduced labour and other input costs (European Commission, 2003h).

These indicators need developing so as to capture, at the level of the firm and locality, the 'complementarities' of the various elements which are key to dynamic change: ICT investment, human skills, organisational change and entrepreneurship (Pettigrew et al, 2003, especially Part 2). The OECD (2003b, ch 3) provides a review of recent studies which demonstrate the importance of these firm-level intersections or complementarities in the context of the new economy: it suggests improved data linking and longitudinal analysis for purposes of developing appropriate indicators (see also US Department of Commerce, 2003; OECD, 2004c). These would be so-called 'third generation' indicators of innovation, based on interactive 'chain-linked' models of innovation, involving feedback loops and organisational as well as technological change (Kline and Rosenberg, 1986; Orsenigo, 2000; Lundvall and Tomlinson, 2002, p 216; ISTAT, 2004, especially pp 37-9, 56).

Finally, it would be good to have indicators which provide insights into the virtuous dynamics by means of which an enterprise, a region or a country can accelerate along the path to a knowledge-based economy, as well as providing early warning of less desirable trajectories. These cumulative processes may need treatment in terms of system dynamics (Checkland and Scholes, 1990; Coyle, 1996; Powell and Bradford, 1998; 2000) and, perhaps, self-organising complex systems (Krugman, 1991). Indicators rooted in these analytical perspectives are still far from well-specified. In practice, we may therefore have to make do with indicators which are very much second-best.

To identify indicators that capture the various elements of this innovation process is no easy matter. If these indicators must also be available in the form of statistics which cover the major industrial countries and are produced on a timely basis, thus allowing for policy benchmarking, the difficulties are accordingly greater. Nevertheless, in the three chapters that follow, we consider what may be possible, in relation to enterprises, human investment and social cohesion respectively.

FIVE

Enterprise and organisational change

Introduction

Our aim is to understand the new knowledge-based economy. However, it is also to identify the major challenges that this economy presents for policy makers and to suggest tools which they might use for monitoring change and for steering social and economic transformation.

Policy makers have hailed the new economy as an engine of dynamism and innovation, productivity growth and competitiveness. Thus, for example, the policy statements developed within the Lisbon process, leading to eEurope 2005, characterise Europe as suffering from a competitiveness gap with the United States and Japan. This is said to arise from an inadequate productivity record, including the use of ICT: "The EU rate of ICT has been gradually rising over the last years from 5.4% of GDP in 1996 to 7.1% of GDP in 2001, almost narrowing the gap with US figures which suffered a marked decline in 2001. However, the increase in ICT spending of the last few years has yet to translate into productivity gains" (European Commission, 2002i). Differences remain in both productivity growth and in levels of investment in ICT, even if within the EU both have been increasing (Jorgensen, 2003a).

Nevertheless, it has long been realised that the connection between ICT investment and productivity is far from simple. Solow's aphorism, "You can see the computer age everywhere but in the productivity statistics" (Solow, 1987), suggested that applying computers to organisations structured and managed in traditional terms would not in itself lead to substantial benefits (see Dedrick et al, 2003, for a survey of the debate). Productivity during the 1980s did increase in most parts of the developed world, but apparently by less among the more intensive users of ICT – services – than in the less intensive users, notably manufacturing (Triplett, 1999). Since then, however, the productivity effects of ICT do seem to be showing through, at least in the US economy. The rapid growth of output per capita in the US during the 1990s has been attributed to the use of ICT to effect qualitative improvements in the performance of companies through business process change, integration of supply chains or substantial reduction of inventory (Triplett, 1999). European business has not apparently been so adept at taking advantage of these opportunities, if formal productivity growth rates are taken into account (albeit some of the difference between the US and the EU is attributable to different conventions for deriving productivity statistics, with the US making greater use of hedonic indicators: as previously discussed in ch 3). This gives weight to the concerns of the European Commission.

Fundamental questions remain, however, about the key variables to be analysed, if we are to understand and measure the processes of innovation within the new economy and their consequences. Within the Lisbon process there is a strong focus on the 'digital economy', echoing the common view that "the 'new economy' refers to the rapid improvements and spread in the use of information and communication technology (ICT), based on computers, software, and communications systems" (Salvatore, 2003). A major aim of EU policy is the roll-out of new technology, with improvements in economic performance and the quality of life expected to come from the breadth

Figure 5.1: Western European ICT market value growth by product segments

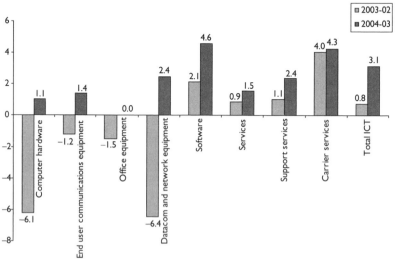

Source: EITO (2004)

of use of ICT and the development of innovative hardware and software. Complementing this is a strong emphasis on technical R&D and its support through fiscal incentives (European Commission, 2003g). This approach is of course not without value. Digital technology can produce major reductions in transaction costs: for example, the provision of real-time information and increased capacity for computation, which allow reduction of inventory levels and the development of just-in-time supply networks. It also permits the supply of digital products (in the entertainment industry for example) through the internet rather than on physical media such as tapes or disks: for these, inventory is simply not required, because the consumer undertakes the copying of the original file. In both cases, the standard definition of a productivity increase, reduction in cost per unit of output, is achieved through the use of ICT.

Nevertheless, this focus on the digital economy tends to divert attention from the organisational and managerial changes that appear to be central to the new economy if the full benefits for competitiveness are to be realised (Farrell, 2003). ICT investments must be combined with "new managerial and organisational techniques and a skilled labour force that gives rise to significant competitiveness improvements" (European Commission, 2000a). These organisational changes are inter-firm as well as intra-firm. In particular, the new knowledge-based economy is a 'network economy', with a premium placed on the exchange of knowledge between organisations, regardless of whether they are part of the same industry or whether, with the spread of electronic communications, they enjoy physical proximity.

This may mean changes in institutional processes at different levels: firm, industry, national economy or international grouping. It also underpins the recognition, in the European Commission's Communication on Innovation Policy (European Commission, 2003c), of the need to link innovation policy to competition, regional, trade and employment policies, and to policies supportive of regional growth nodes and 'industrial districts' (European Commission, 2003g; De Panizza and Fazio, 2004).

It is to a deeper and more theoretically informed understanding of organisational change that we now turn, before applying our conceptual understanding of innovation in the new economy.

Organisational change in relation to technology and performance

Major changes are under way in the organisational forms which enterprises adopt. Many of these are rendered possible by the new information technologies, but they may in turn have significant consequences for the way that these technologies are then used, and the consequences for productivity and competitiveness.

One review of the research literature on innovative forms of organising has identified three key themes (Pettigrew and Massini, 2003): the globalising firm and its changing boundaries; the knowledge firm in the knowledge economy; networks and the socially-embedded firm. The INNFORM (Innovative Forms of Organising) programme, within which this review took place, then identifies nine indicators of organisational innovation, referring to structures, processes and boundaries (Figure 5.1). The indicators are derived from surveys of enterprises in the US, Western Europe and Japan during the 1990s.[1] They are organised in relation to:

- *Changing structures*: Heavy hierarchical layers of middle management are under dual pressure – they are too expensive and they impede information flows and quickness of response. Decentralisation promotes cross-functional and cross-boundary teams and more flexible, project-based organisation structures.
- *Changing processes*: The knowledge economy is characterised by intensive interaction and communication, which requires new investments in ICT. Intra-firm flows of information are horizontal, promoting co-adaptive exploitation and cross-boundary synergies. Further, the flows of information are moving outward to include customers and suppliers. Human resource management takes on a strategic importance as companies recognise people – and the knowledge they carry – as key resources.
- *Changing boundaries*: As companies focus on core competencies and a narrower span of activity, there is pressure to shift towards smaller, decentralised units. Hierarchy and scale can impede the flexibility needed in hypercompetitive environments, so firms outsource value chain activities of low perceived value, as well as non-core activities such as training and research and development. Firms make increased use of strategic alliances to supplement their own competencies. These new and more flexible organisational architectures make for a 'network economy'.

Figure 5.2: New forms of organising: multiple indicators

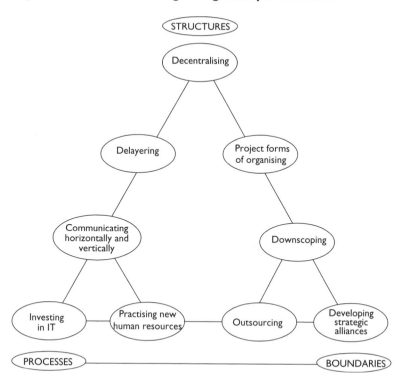

Source: Pettigrew et al (2003)

Pettigrew and Massini (2003) take a holistic approach to the framework, arguing that it is not enough to look at the nine indicators independently. They draw on Milgrom and Roberts (1995), arguing that while high-performing firms are commonly combining a number of innovative practices at the same time, organisational change in just a few dimensions may lead to negative payoffs. In other words, there seems to be a J-curve relationship between change and performance outcome: where implementation is only partial, this may make things worse. These complementarities traps may then help to explain the slow diffusion of best practice across industries and nations. They also, however, stress that system benefits will depend upon the national context: what we earlier referred to as the national innovation system (Massini and Pettigrew, 2003, p 170).

The introduction of information systems is therefore not itself enough to change or develop organisations. There needs to be alignment between the business strategy, technology, organisational structure, management processes and the roles and skills of people in the organisation (Scott Morton, 1991). This type of innovation – the adoption of new technologies, new working practices, and new forms of organising – has been examined in depth by Rogers (2003). He points to the importance for innovation of a non-bureaucratic and informal ethos within an organisation. However, more than this he reports that the innovativeness of an organisation is consistently and positively related to its size. The latter is a surrogate for a number of hidden variables, such as employees' technical expertise, organisational structure and, most of all, 'organisational slack', which Rogers defines as "the degree to which uncommitted resources are available to an organisation" (p 412). This suggests that SMEs (small and medium sized enterprises) may face serious constraints on their ability to innovate successfully.

Stage 1: Preparation and invention

Enterprises scan the challenges presented by the new information technologies. They take stock of their capacities to respond to these challenges, but also the resources that are available to them in the wider society, through the national, European and international innovation systems. They devise inventive responses in the light of available leading edge practice. However, the extent to which enterprises undertake these activities varies greatly.

An important capacity in organisations is the awareness among managers of the potential benefits and limits of investment in ICT. This has been highlighted by successive investigations into business information systems, as a key factor in avoiding the failure of ICT investment, when costs outrunning benefits are common (Strassman, 1985; Powell, 1992; Smith and Keil, 2003). However, it is also important for innovation that the variety of potential uses of ICT should be appreciated, so that applications of the technology are not confined to the familiar and well-understood. At the same time, innovation in the organisation need not involve the most recent advances in computing. Where innovations such as process development and electronic commerce have been influential, they have often used technologies such as relational databases that are well-understood and well-established in themselves, but which are being used in new ways.

This suggests that in order to capture the key elements within Stage 1, indicators are needed of:

- the knowledge management systems that organisations have in place to scan, learn and plan;
- resources for invention and innovation;

- outputs from invention into subsequent stages of the innovation process.

Knowledge management systems

The literature on the new economy highlights the more rapid diffusion of global best-technology practice and processes of learning-by-doing. The former is at the heart of discussions of knowledge management, with enterprises and governments scanning the globe for best practice, new opportunities and impending threats. This is learning-by-scanning. Learning-by-doing raises questions as to the capacity of organisations to adapt to, and exploit, new technologies and production processes, in order to gain competitive advantage.

Organisations do not limit their searches to inventions occurring in their home country or region. Largely because of the dramatic improvements in world-wide communication which ICTs have enabled, the knowledge bases that are relevant to both technical and organisational innovation are now essentially global. Much corporate R&D is conducted across continents by multinational enterprises. In the case of global ICT companies it is hard to disentangle the contribution of particular national or regional innovation systems: the major US corporations such as IBM and Hewlett-Packard have for several decades included European sites within their R&D effort (Buderi, 2000). This globalisation of the ICT industry produces some curious anomalies: "the side-by-side occurrence of world-class US IT-producing companies and the nation's chronic deficit in IT goods trade appears to be largely a result of the globalisation of the production and distribution of IT goods and services" (US Department of Commerce, 2003).

The global nature of R&D in this area is illustrated by the pioneers of enterprise resource planning systems. These left IBM's German research facility to found SAP, only then to see their software being applied most publicly in the United States, as the foundation of cross-functional information systems on which the redesign of processes could take place (Davenport, 2000). As foreseen therefore in our conceptual discussion (see Chapter 4), the various stages of innovation that we have distinguished unfold within a complex international division of intellectual labour.

To measure and monitor this trade in knowledge – especially inside multinational organisations – is however extremely difficult, part of the larger challenge of conceptualising and measuring 'intangibles' in the knowledge-based economy. Indicators of these knowledge-related intangibles are difficult to operationalise, since existing accounting structures are commonly delimited by national boundaries, whereas knowledge may inhere in multinational teams (Eustace, 2004a).

Resources for invention and innovation

Invention and innovation depend in part on the resources that enterprises can draw down from the national, European and international innovation systems. Indicators are readily available of R&D spending and of the proportion of science and technology graduates within the graduate population for different countries. These are however rather broad in scope: it may therefore be useful also to take the proportion of high-skilled ICT workers, rather than high-skilled workers in general.

The national innovation system also involves a wide range of 'knowledge institutions', which interact with enterprises in knowledge-intensive communities of practice, involving both users and producers of innovation. Potentially relevant indicators include those dealing with research spin-offs (Lehtoranta, 2004), knowledge flows (Statistics Finland, 2004b) and innovation processes (Wolters, 2003a). Other possible indicators of know-how inputs could include previous patents acquired, licences held to use other's research, and R&D networking (for example, as between public and private sectors, educational and other sectors, military and non-military sectors).[2]

Figure 5.3: Business R&D expenditure (BERD) (% of GDP)

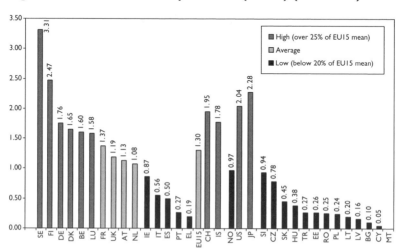

Source: European Commission (2003h)

Indicators of the amount of high-tech venture capital investment are often taken as showing the propensity of different countries to develop advanced technology. However, the focus is, again, rather broad and these indicators tend not to capture the links with the new information technologies. Indicators are also of course available showing the extent to which enterprises are endowed with ICT equipment and connected to the internet. These have some value as measures of technical readiness, even if they are of rather limited value in relation to the *uses* to which these technologies are put.

None of these indicators, however, cover the type of applied knowledge that needs to be generated, if ICT is to be linked to organisational change. Indicators of the extent and effectiveness of managerial innovation are particularly hard to define. Business plans are not currently subject to the same intellectual property regime as technical innovation, which means that there is not the same kind of central register that exists for patents (May, 2000). Most of the ideas on which businesses draw for guiding ICT-enabled change exist in the public domain, in books, journals and the internet. However, where successful projects have led to productivity increases, the precise details of how the general ideas have been applied is often a matter of commercial confidence.

There is also a dearth of indicators concerned with the attitudes of senior management towards organisational change. While the literature on ICT investment emphasises the importance of their commitment, in aligning the technological, informational and organisational requirements of change (eg Scott Morton, 1991), the available indicators do little to address this. Within Europe at least, much of the available survey data are more concerned with their perceptions of the external opportunities offered by the new economy, notably the importance of e-business (BISER, 2004a). In relation to ICT investment and organisational change, a start has been made by surveys for projects such as INNFORM and EBIP, but more work is needed to generate larger data sets (see OECD, 2002a; Pettigrew et al, 2003).

Outputs from invention

Outputs from R&D are most commonly measured by reference to the numbers of patents applied for, and the number of innovating enterprises which make applications. Nevertheless, patent measures have well-known deficiencies. One is that patenting by multinational corporations may be a poor indicator of where within its multinational activities an enterprise is conducting its innovative activities. A second

Figure 5.4: Patents granted at the US Patents and Trademark Office relative to GDP by country of inventor (1999)

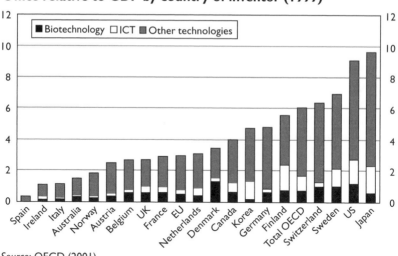

Source: OECD (2001)

difficulty is the lack of cross-national comparability, with indicators of patent uptake in Europe and the US distorted by differences in patent law. The EU is considering reform of its patent law to extend the scope of ICT-related innovation, so as to embrace business methods, in line with US law (Hart et al, 2001).

A third difficulty is that patenting may be undertaken defensively, in order to protect market positions. Thus, for example, the German company SAP, discussed above, which dominates the market for Enterprise Resource Planning (ERP) applications, began to apply for such patents in 1999: for example in systems for value chain optimisation. By this time, however, SAP had been in existence and involved in substantial R&D for 20 years: patent applications were adopted as a defence mechanism against the use of patents by US firms to appropriate areas of the ERP market, rather than as the preferred intellectual property strategy (http://swpat.ffii.org/akteure/sap/).

As an indicator of invention activity, the number of patents may have more merit in hardware than in software. Patent-related knowledge is often not applicable to the kind of organisational change that leads to process improvement: the latter typically involving a form of 'learning-by-doing', in which the key ideas relate to the application of technology rather than to the technology itself. The difficulty lies not only in determining whether or not such inventive activity is taking place, but also in evaluating its impact. For the application of ICT to organisational activity the process is harder to detect, because the type of knowledge is applied rather than theoretical, and transmitted informally rather than through registration of patents.

Stage 2: Application

Enterprises select inventions generated at Stage 1 and apply these in a process of learning-by-doing. These application activities can include advances in information technologies, involving increased power of computation, wider incorporation of existing technology into intermediate and final products, and new digital products. They can also include new organisational forms enabled by ICT, including e-commerce and new configurations of intra- and interorganisational activity.

Technological and organisational changes are usually both involved. They can however take a variety of forms: technology rarely entirely dictates what these should be. At the same time, unlike advances in algorithm design or processor power, the effectiveness of organisational changes may vary according to cultural, economic and historical factors, both of the organisation and of the environment in which it operates. This further complicates the process of devising indicators on a cross-European basis.

Advances in information technologies

Advances in information technologies may involve improvements in the power and quality of some component or final product – for example, in the processing speed and memory capacity of silicon chips and PCs, in line with what has become known as Moore's Law. This can be thought of as a 'vertical' or quality-ladder process. Analytically distinct from this is the 'horizontal' process of variety expansion, with growing differentiation in the range of products embodying ICT, putting dedicated computational capacity into more and more intermediate inputs and final outputs, and moving away from a generic free-standing computer. This is closely related to the notion of 'recombinant innovation' as a key driver in the ICT sector: the underlying components can be permuted in many different ways (Varian, 2000), as for example in the permutations of telecommunications, information-processing and presentation in mobile phones.

Indicators of these two dimensions of technological advance are

Figure 5.5: A large ICT hardware sector does not guarantee rapid MFP growth

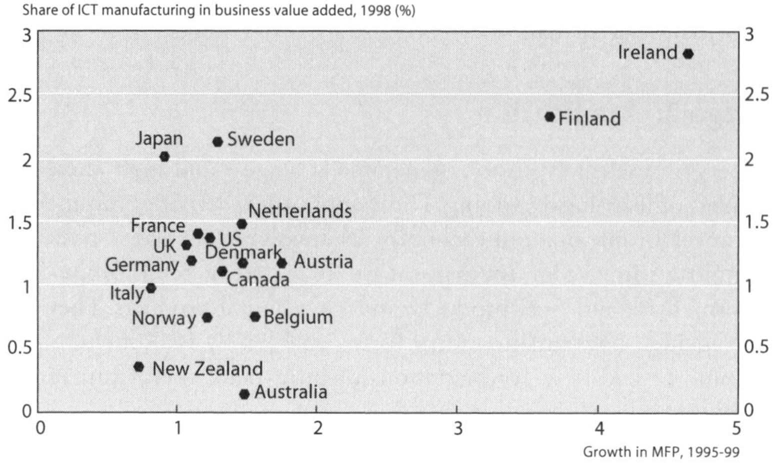

Share of ICT manufacturing in business value added, 1998 (%)

Growth in MFP, 1995-99

Source: OECD (2001)

difficult to select and the available statistical materials are somewhat limited. Indicators of the levels of employment in the ICT-producing sectors, or the numbers of enterprises, may give some very general picture of the scale of this sector in the country concerned: we know that size is broadly related to innovative capacity, so this may also indicate the pace at which 'vertical' improvements in quality may be proceeding. However, what we also know is that a country does not by any means need to produce ICT itself – certainly not hardware – in order for its enterprises to reap major benefits from ICT-related organisational innovation (OECD, 2001).

Indicators relating to the 'horizontal' spread of innovation across product categories are also sparse. An exception is the OECD's detailed analysis of software – and the rate of improvement in the quality of specific products (OECD, 2002f, ch 3).

New organisational forms enabled by ICT

Any investigation of application activity will need to pay particular attention to the pioneer organisations where experimentation is most likely to take place. These are not necessarily those containing formal R&D departments, but rather those who engage in strategic thinking as to the ways in which their ICT resources should be used. As seen earlier in this chapter, there is plenty of evidence that it is larger organisations that that have the resource base to embark on the development of new information systems: size matters, and in particular 'organisational slack'. This makes it hard for SMEs to be prime movers at this stage of innovation (their significance at subsequent stages in the innovation process is discussed later).

As noted in Chapter 4, the European Innovation Scoreboard includes indicators of the proportion of SMEs that are involved in product and process innovation (either in-house or in cooperation with others) and the proportion of innovative enterprises that are able thereby to reinforce their position, in terms of increased market share or reduced labour and other input costs (European Commission, 2003h). These need developing into more sophisticated surveys and indicators, applied not to SMEs but the larger enterprises that are the main drivers of innovation. This will need to be combined with assessments of the relative positions of such companies within different sectors and industries, to see if the more innovative organisations are gaining market share within the domestic, European or global economy: in other words to estimate the impact of such innovations where they exist.

We can pose two questions. First, to what extent are enterprises undertaking organisational innovations which apply ICT in novel ways? Second, what are the benefits and impact of such innovations for the organisations concerned?

Extent of organisational innovation

There are well-established statistics of ICT expenditure in different countries, but these will not necessarily cover innovative applications of ICT to forms of organisation. Increases in ICT expenditure can even mask patterns of use that obstruct innovation, as for example with the concentration before 2000 on the 'millennium bug', which produced rapid increases in corporate ICT budgets, but subsequent contraction.

A complement to this kind of data is the survey of managerial practices of the type performed in the INNFORM survey (Pettigrew et al, 2003). Here firms are questioned about their adoption of changes to processes and structures, of the kind which seem to produce improved performance in the new economy: for example, enterprise resource planning systems, supply chain management, customer relations management and knowledge management. For analytical purposes, however, these need to be isolated from the more conventional processing of operational data. There is of course a danger in prejudging the type of innovation that should be monitored, since this may obscure the innovative nature of the new economy, in which

Figure 5.6: New work practices and ICT investment

1996 ICT expenditures (% of GDP)

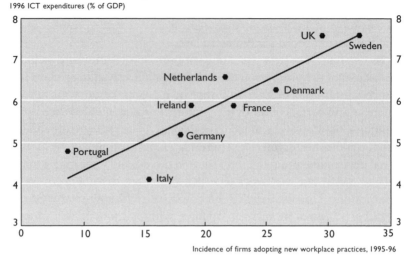

Incidence of firms adopting new workplace practices, 1995-96

Source: OECD (2001)

experimentation with new technologies produces new uses which are essentially unpredictable. Those applications which are currently associated with innovation and enhanced performance may well become routine and unexceptional.

Benefits of organisational innovation

It is nevertheless possible to draw on recent studies of business practices to decide on the types of application that are producing benefits. The difficulty is to produce statistically significant results. Various EU research projects bring together case studies which provide an illuminating picture of organisations gaining a variety of benefits from ICT investments (see, for example, BEEP, 2002). These are a good way of capturing the richness of situations in which there are multiple factors contributing to the success or failure of a project. However, the nature of this information is episodic: extremely useful as exemplars, but not necessarily representative of industry across Europe and rarely amenable to the gathering of statistical data.

Statistics are available about the extent of e-commerce markets, both business-to-consumer and business-to-business (BISER, 2003). However, while this is clearly an important part of the new economy, it does not cover all possible uses of information technology that have an impact on working practices within companies, organisational performance and productivity. Nonetheless, these statistics are worth collecting as comparative indicators of the levels of uptake of a form of ICT usage which is leading to changing practices in large parts of the European economy.

Productivity levels can be compared among developed countries. These statistics can then be linked to data on levels of ICT investment, to establish where ICT is being used to greatest benefit. This type of assessment provides useful backdrop for considering the effectiveness of new investments: nevertheless, it does not distinguish between more and less innovative uses of ICT, nor does it illuminate precisely how ICT contributes to improved performance. A step forward is offered by the *Digital Economy* reports, where explicit links are made between the adoption of integrated enterprise resource planning applications and improved performance reports (US Department of Commerce, 2003). The comparison here is between the advanced use of ICT and the basic use of standard packages: computerisation on its own is not an indicator of innovation, in a world in which computers are becoming commonplace.

What is needed is a mix of coarse- and fine-grained measures. The former would assess overall levels of ICT investment and the impact on levels of productivity. The fine-grained indicators would assess the take-up of innovative practices by companies: examples would currently include enterprise resource planning systems and ICT applications for supply chain and customer relations management. This would, however, require regular review, so as to take account of changes to both technology and the uses to which it is put.

Stage 3: Diffusion

We start with the rate of diffusion of knowledge-based innovations, both technological and organisational, across the economy generally. We then examine the factors affecting the absorptive capacity of the SME sector in particular. Finally, we look at the consequences for the overall organisational reconfiguration of the economy.

As far as the diffusion of specific technologies is concerned, indicators are fairly readily available, showing the intensity of ICT-usage by industrial sector and how this is changing over time. They include indicators of economy-wide ICT infrastructure provision, business sector ICT capacity and usage, and employment involving ICT applications. It is important to track these changes, although particular indicators will lose resonance as diffusion widens and deepens. We have however stressed that at least as important are the ICT-enabled changes that take place within the internal processes of organisations.

Figure 5.7: Internet penetration by activity, 2002 or latest available year: Percentage of businessess with 10 or more employees using the internet

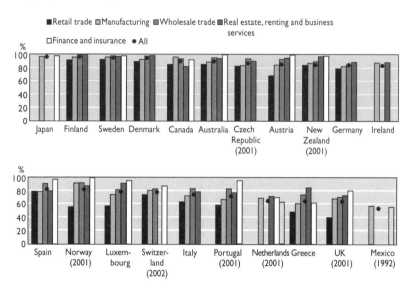

Source: OECD (2003a)

The diffusion of novel organisational forms is therefore of equal analytical and policy interest. As yet there are however no systematic instruments for tracking these processes on a cross-national basis.

Scope for diffusion across the SME sector

At Stage 2 we referred to pioneer organisations in areas of information usage and management change. Much, though not necessarily all, of the innovation that leads to improved organisational performance is developed in and/or for large, private-sector companies. These are the organisations with the resources to fund large, risky projects and they also work on a scale which makes the integration of their internal processes – or between themselves and their customers or suppliers – a particularly pressing problem.

However, the diffusion of productivity-enhancing technologies and techniques, to an extent that would produce substantial national or pan-European shifts in productivity, requires the spread of these innovations to sectors of the economy that do not have the same level of resources for ICT investment: whether in the public, voluntary or

SME sectors. This spread of competitiveness-enhancing innovations from the pioneer firms to the wider economy can involve the wholesale transplantation of particular types of information system, but more common is the adaptation of practices to particular circumstances. While larger companies can support the development of custom-made, bespoke applications, the spread of innovations to smaller companies is relatively piecemeal, involving ad hoc use of whatever links and standard packages are available, rather than long-term investment in custom-built solutions (Naylor and Williams, 1994).

We concentrate in this section therefore on the use of ICT innovations by the SME sector, which in all economies form the majority of enterprises, and are particularly important as generators of new employment. SMEs are commonly thought to be flexible and innovative organisations, able to respond quickly to customer and market demands. However, SME strategies tend to be emergent, informal and medium-term rather than long-term (Hadjimanolis, 2000). They concentrate upon differentiating their product or service from those already in the market: this may enable them to grow successfully, as they exploit a gap in the market (Hay and Kamshad, 1994). Such planning as they undertake is operational rather than strategic, the main objective being to provide the product or service efficiently and effectively (Hagmann and Mccahon, 1993).

SMEs typically have small product runs. This makes for a sort of flexibility, enabling them to respond quickly to customer and market demands. As seen above, however, the kind of innovation in processes and structures associated with benefit from ICT requires organisational

Figure 5.8: Proportion of enterprises with innovation activity, EU, 1998-2000 (%)

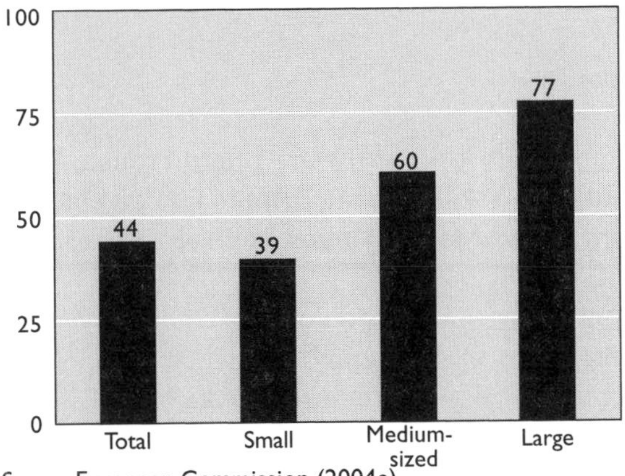

Source: European Commission (2004e)

Figure 5.9: Proportion of enterprises implementing advanced management techniques, EU, 1998-2000 (%)

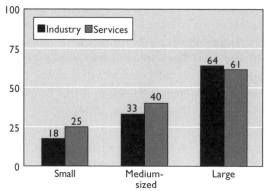

Source: European Commission (2004e)

Figure 5.10: Proportion of enterprises implementing new or significantly changed organisational structures, EU, 1998-2000 (%)

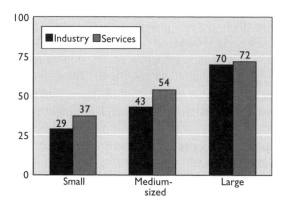

Source: European Commission (2004e)

slack, something which SMEs lack. SMEs are often resource-poor not only financially, but also in skills, forcing them to rely on external consultants. Continuing innovation is therefore unlikely (Keasey and Watson, 1994).

Faced with these constraints, the diffusion of new competitiveness-enhancing innovations, across the economy as a whole, is likely to depend upon the technological infrastructure to which SMEs have access; the availability of advanced business process packages in standardised forms which mimic on a smaller scale the kind of specialised cross-organisational systems which larger firms can afford; networks of inter-firm support which can surmount the limitations of their small size; and appropriate human resources and training. In short, the national – and European – innovation system needs to be SME-friendly. Appropriate support of these different sorts can serve as a proxy for the 'organisational slack' identified by Rogers (2003) as being necessary for the diffusion of innovation. This can be provided externally, by the state or by commercial contractors. Alternatively, it can be generated by networks of enterprises acting collectively.

Without the organisational slack to invest in corporate networks, SMEs are particularly dependent on pre-existing technological infrastructure. Good indicators are available, principally from Eurostat, for assessing the extent of such support, in terms of broadband access and the speed of electronic communication (European Commission, 2003g). The availability and use of these infrastructures varies, however, according to location. While the developed world has ready access to telephony, for much of the developing world the supply of electricity and data communications are erratic and sometimes non-existent. Even within the industrialised world there are urban-rural differences (BISER, 2004b). However, in countries such as Canada, government support for their extension into rural areas is encouraging businesses to relocate to rural and less developed areas. This has important potential implications for rural development and social inclusion (discussed later in Chapter 7).

Access to technology is only the first step towards using it for improved performance. Innovative applications are required to run on it and people need to be trained to use them. Complete systems for enterprise resource planning or supply chain management are unlikely to be feasible for SMEs. However, smaller-scale and more standardised versions of such innovative approaches are possible. For example, Telefónica, the principal Spanish telecommunications firm, provides EDI links for small firms, using a web-based facility. The connections created are not as specific to the companies' requirements as would be the case in a customised application; nevertheless, they allow SMEs to develop the kind of electronic connections to suppliers and customers that can support their continued participation in markets where rapid communications and reduced transactions costs are becoming essential. It would be useful to monitor the availability and take-up of this sort of service. There are of course indicators of the size of the ICT market in different countries, but these are too broad: more fruitful would be indicators of those parts of the ICT industry that provide standardised versions of advanced systems: what are known as application service providers (ASPs) (Fantasia, 2000).

Networks of enterprises are also important in providing support for SMEs, as they adopt new technologies and corresponding new organisational forms. Indeed, their survival and prosperity often depends on the alliances they strike with larger sector leaders (Lehtoranta, 2004). Such alliances are also however in the interests of those larger players, consistent with the new organisational configurations which we traced earlier in this chapter, involving outsourcing and more flexible boundaries in the network economy. Further research is needed on the support which networks can provide within the competitive environment of the new economy. Indicators of innovation intensity within such networks are being developed and could be used to indicate the development of cross-organisational slack (De Panizza et al, 2004).

Finally, the diffusion of innovations depends on appropriate human resources. While people who are involved in invention and initial application are often based in organisations with a considerable body of technical skills and expertise, those outside these pioneering sectors will often have to develop skills from scratch. One way of addressing this would be to examine the spread of ICT knowledge through formal training programmes. Europe is particularly well-endowed with traditions of vocational education, compared to other parts of the developed world. In the European Computer Driving License (ECDL), for example, it has a computer literacy qualification which is being widely taken up by employers in the private and public sectors as a benchmark indicator of proficiency. To add to its attractions for comparative analysis, its curriculum and assessment are standard across the Continent and the registration is centralised in national accreditation bodies such as the British Computer Society. In principle, therefore, collecting data on the extent and growth of qualifications such as ECDL would be feasible.

Such data should be used with caution, however. The relevance of standardised computer literacy programmes in the dynamic and unpredictable environment of the new economy is questionable. A highly specific and predetermined course in standard software packages may be insufficient to equip employees for the flexibility and initiative they are expected to show in contemporary organisations, as the literature on 'information literacy' demonstrates (Mutch, 1997; Bruce, 1999). On the other hand, competence in familiar forms of software can at least provide a foundation from which further exploration can proceed.

Overall organisational reconfiguration of the economy

As far as the general transformation of social institutions and markets is concerned, some indicators are available, including the volume of e-commerce and the proportion of teleworkers (BISER, 2004a; 2004e). This is of obvious importance, given the increased competitiveness of industries in which large numbers of transactions are online or where business-to-business e-commerce is significant. Fewer indicators are available that might reveal how the new forms of organising at the level of the enterprise (in terms of changing structures, processes and boundaries: see Figure 5.1 above), coupled with the new institutional ecologies within which MNEs and SMEs find themselves, issue in new and powerful configurations at the level of society and economy as a whole.

As seen earlier in this chapter, it is common for individual enterprises to forge strategic alliances with partners located variously across the local, national, European and global economies, extending their boundaries and supplementing their own core competencies. The challenge is to understand how these processes develop and to suggest indicators of relevance to policy makers who wish to support them. One approach is in terms of indicators of business demography: the birth of new firms – including spin-offs – and their eventual deaths. With the increasing fuzziness of organisational boundaries and the volatility of new enterprises, especially in the high-tech sectors of the economy, this is no easy matter. Statistics Finland has sought to distinguish 'real' births from restructuring of existing activities using various forms of data triangulation. Work of this sort is essential for illuminating the transformation dynamics of the new knowledge-based economy (Lehtoranta, 2004).

Just as important is to understand how the dynamics of increasing external returns in the new economy can lead to general organisational reconfiguration across the economy as a whole. Such increasing external returns were acknowledged in the previous chapter, as a key element of the network economy. As we also noted, much of the discussion of such returns has historically been in the context of regional agglomeration. In the new knowledge-based economy, however, the revolution in communications makes spatial proximity less significant for the enjoyment of these returns and facilitates the development of global value chains. At the leading edge of attempts to develop indicators of these wider organisational transformations, therefore, are studies which bring together the local and global dimensions of the network economy within this analytical framework of increasing external returns.

The G-NIKE Project (Growth-Nodes in a Knowledge-Based Europe) is one such attempt: a European Commission sponsored project, investigating regional and interregional ICT-enabled 'growth nodes'. Its aim was to shed new light on how and why growth nodes emerge and to examine the policy implications (O'Callaghan, 2004). The growth node concept of the G-NIKE project is grounded in complex adaptive systems theory: it considers growth within the context of the internal and external connectivity of a self-organising system. It focuses attention on the positive synergies that can be achieved between dynamic social networks at the local level – involving, for example, transaction support, business processes and community building – and the global interconnectedness afforded by ICT, stimulating external connectivity through knowledge management and learning processes (see also, for example, recent work by ISTAT, concerned with the reconfiguration of regional clusters and value chains in Italy: De Panizza et al, 2004).

Stage 4: Outcomes

From the point of view of public policy, what is of interest is the contribution of innovation to productivity growth and competitiveness. The policy goals are that European companies should take advantage of ICTs to increase productivity (whether by emulating the practices of US companies or by adapting the use of information systems to specifically European conditions) and to improve their competitive position, not simply passing productivity increases on to consumers through lower prices, but also improving their use of data to understand their customers and develop new products and ways of working. This improved competitiveness should then be manifest in improved market share in the information–intensive industries, compared to firms from the other major industrial economies. For Europe to surpass the US in productivity growth would not be unprecedented: it would merely resume the trend that was evident in at least some parts of the EU during the 1960s and 1970s. In a longer-term historical perspective, leadership of a wave of technological innovation is rarely sustained in the long term, as follower economies develop the skills to participate and overtake the pioneers.

If policy interventions are to enhance the contribution of innovation to competitiveness, they must take into account the specific features of the new economy highlighted in the foregoing pages. Innovation, as we have seen, involves not only the application of new technologies, but also the development of new organisational forms, with corresponding changes in management and in workforce skills. In turn, these transformations presuppose 'organisational slack' or proxies thereof, in the form of a national and European innovation system which is supportive of SMEs, as they seek to exploit the opportunities offered by the new economy. These supports need not be directly provided by governments: the existence of networks of companies that provide mutual support, of e-marketplaces which facilitate the development of links between businesses, and of standardised forms of innovative information system are all worth monitoring, even if they arise from spontaneous private sector activity.

It follows that policy recommendations and interventions are insufficient if, like those emanating from the Lisbon process, they concentrate on the provision of standards and targets for the roll-out of electronic communications, chiefly broadband, and the provision of tax incentives for formal research and development. While these are helpful, they do not address the full scale of managerial and organisational change that is necessary to achieve competitiveness benefits. Policy should address wider questions of the adaptation of information systems to organisational needs and circumstances. To produce indicators of the consequences of innovation – technological and organisational – for productivity and competitiveness is however no easy matter, especially if such indicators are to be used for comparing performance in different countries. It is equally difficult to move from the sometimes rather general assessments of the innovation process traced in the foregoing pages to develop more precise guidelines for policy.

Indicators of productivity and competitiveness in relation to innovation

The OECD (2002d; 2003b) and the US Department of Commerce (2003) have each devoted considerable resources to producing comparative data on the uses made of ICT in different countries and their impact on productivity. These provide estimates of how productivity and ICT usage have changed over time, disaggregated by industry and sector. Also of value is the work of Brynjolfsson and Hitt (1996), who collected survey data from firms comparing overall labour productivity with the level of ICT investment. They concluded that the 'productivity paradox' was on its way to being overcome, with the productivity effects of ICT showing through as business processes

Figure 5.11: The contribution of ICT-using services to aggregate productivity growth

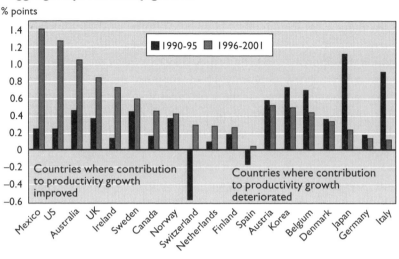

Source: OECD (2003b)

were transformed. There remains however the caveat, noted by the OECD, that "ICT's impact remains difficult to capture ... in many service sectors, due to (well known) problems in the measurement of output" (OECD, 2003b).

A further step is to examine how the heavier ICT-using industries in Europe are performing in their global markets. Changes in the market share of whole industries provide one relevant measure. Further work is needed on detecting the extent to which ICT-related innovation supports competitive position in ways more sensitive than pure market share (see also Figure 4.4 above). Productivity and competitiveness are however by no means synonymous and competitiveness can arise from different forms of strategy. While some firms will follow the classic path of using productivity gains to pass efficiencies on to customers in the form of lower prices (a 'cost leadership' approach), others follow a different path. As noted above, SMEs often adopt a differentiation strategy, developing additional features of their products to distinguish them in the market place. The Electronic Commerce Business Impacts Project (EBIP) survey contains questions about the contribution of ICT to competitiveness, in an effort to distinguish these different strategies (OECD, 2002a).

Nevertheless, in all of these cases the focus is on ICT use and investment, without reference to the organisational forms within which ICT is deployed and the contribution of management and workforce skills. It is not just that these additional elements of the innovation process need to be taken into account. It is also that new organisational forms – for example, the development of networks that cut across industries and regions – may make it more difficult to identify the relevant organisational units, complicating the assessment of outcomes. The G-NIKE project illustrates the effort to develop indicators that capture networks and growth-nodes of this sort, with a view to generating policy making support tools for assessing regional and local support for networks (O'Callaghan, 2004).

Guidelines for policy intervention

The impact of policy itself on the new economy is being addressed in business-level surveys such as EBIP (OECD, 2002a), collecting data about the perceived effectiveness of regulations and the provision of vocational education. Systematic use of such data would however require triangulation with more sophisticated instruments of analysis, if the impact of policy decisions at firm level is to be assessed. More fundamentally, however, the very rapidity of change in the new economy means that policy may forever lag behind. Although the present discussion has used such application types as ERP or CRM systems as examples of innovative linkages between ICT and organisational needs, there may come a time when they are either outdated or universal, and when attention will have to shift to new forms of information system. It is therefore important, in analysing the effectiveness of policy decisions, to monitor the continuing salience of the indicators themselves, in conditions of rapid change. Regular investigation of important new developments, of the kind pioneered by the BEEP case studies (BEEP, 2002) would help to establish the categories which should be captured by indicators.

Conclusion

At the end of the Chapter 4, we considered what sort of indicators policy makers may need in order to monitor and steer the new economy. The discussion of the present chapter has confirmed that particularly common are indicators referring to the technological capacity and human resources of different countries: aspects of their 'readiness' for innovation. Also common are indicators which capture the spread of particular technological innovations across the economy and society.

In concluding Chapter 4 we argued, however, that while these latter indicators reveal the extent to which the innovation has penetrated even to the laggards, what was important for policy makers was also to have indicators of the 'leading edge' of invention and application. These indicators would measure how significant within the sector or country concerned were enterprises which are generating new innovations: and they would capture how successive waves of innovation reinforce the position of those first able to ride them. In the present chapter, notably at Stage 2, we have made some use of the European Innovation Scoreboard indicators, showing the proportions of innovative enterprises and the extent to which this innovation consolidates their market position. We have also however pointed to the need to elaborate these indicators, so as to capture the specific types of innovation – technological and organisational – which are associated with such benefits. In relation to SMEs, we have also set innovation in the context of a user-friendly regional and national innovation system, and analysed the various aspects of this user-friendliness for which indicators can be developed.

Chapter 4 argued that beyond this, what was ideally required was indicators which captured the intersections and 'complementarities' of the ICT investment, human skills, organisational change and entrepreneurship which together make for dynamic innovation and transformation in the new economy: intersections, moreover, at the level of the individual organisation, rather than just national indicators for each of these elements taken separately. These would be so-called 'third generation' indicators of innovation, based on interactive 'chain-linked' models of innovation, involving feedback loops and organisational as well as technological change. In the present chapter we have seen that available indicators provide fragmented glimpses of these complementarities, notably through our discussion of the G-NIKE project and the INNFORM survey. These are not without interest for policy makers, but they are hardly sufficient for an information-based society that expects to rely on evidence-based policies.

What may therefore be needed is a new, validated survey instrument of innovation in organisational forms. It would need also to investigate enabling and constraining factors in the environment of enterprises, such as the ICT infrastructure and availability of required skills. The survey data could then be subjected to econometric analysis, mapping the results to traditional measures of performance, such as return on capital employed. This would help to answer in objective terms the question of whether or not the gains in competitiveness predicted for the organisational innovations were actually materialising. The key outcome of this process would be the linkage of survey and qualitative data with larger-scale statistical analysis, areas of data collection which are currently separate. The survey would also, however, need to be backed up with in-depth case studies to explore emerging themes and trends and to establish which types of change were most significant at the time, offering greatest potential for enhanced performance.

This might then also begin to address our final plea in Chapter 4: for indicators which could provide insights into the virtuous dynamics by which an enterprise, a region or a country can accelerate along the path to a knowledge-based economy, as well as providing early warning of less desirable trajectories. Such trajectories depend upon the national and European innovation and regulatory systems in which enterprises are embedded: indicators of dynamics must also therefore capture the characteristics of these systems. It is after all primarily by nudging these systems, rather than by seeking to act directly on enterprises themselves, that policy makers can shape trajectories of socio-economic development. Armed with such indicators, we may then also be in a position to re-examine the stability issues raised in Chapter 3 – but now within a dynamic frame of reference. That is however beyond the scope of the present work.

SIX

Human investment and learning

Introduction

Human investment is central to the new knowledge-based economy. In Chapter 4, for example, we saw that human capital occupies a key role within recent neo-Schumpeterian growth theory; and that sociological models of organisational learning give a central place to 'communities of practice' which apply skills of practical creativity. Chapter 5, concerned with organisational change, identified the skills of those working at different levels within an organisation as the necessary complement to ICT investment, business strategy and managerial leadership, in securing the dynamics of innovation.

The new economy generates new requirements for human capital and skills, so that the workforce can deal effectively with technological innovation in ICT and with organisational transformation, both in the economy and in public services. This changes the outputs expected from education and training institutions. At the same time, however, these institutions are themselves exploiting the new technologies and they are developing novel organisational and market strategies, in an effort to shape and to benefit from the opportunities which the new economy affords. Finally, of course, these developments also transform the situation in which individuals and households find themselves: the range of skills that are in demand on the job market, the opportunities for learning and the sources of information, by means of which they can make decisions on education and training, and judge the costs and benefits of those decisions.

These transformations are taking place across a global terrain. While the global diffusion of advances in technology and business processes is nothing new, the pace is accelerating, with education and training services themselves subject to these globalising tendencies. The ICT revolution is one contributing element: there are of course others, notably the political drive for open markets under the auspices of the WTO, including GATS (Knight, 2003). Education and training systems are no longer a secure part of domestic national policy (although national independence of education and training regimes prior to the present century can be exaggerated: see Room, 2002). However, the direction and extent of these pressures of globalisation are not uniform: they are shaped by the specific political economies of the countries and regions involved and the position they occupy within the global distribution of economic and cultural power (for further discussion, see for example Cornford and Pollock, 2003).

The Lisbon Summit looked to a knowledge-based economy giving a central place to skills, education and training. This emphasis has been echoed and reinforced in a wide variety of policy statements and studies emanating from the EU institutions. The *e*Europe Action Plan (European Council and European Commission, 2000) and its accompanying benchmark indicators have been introduced already: so has the drive for a European Research Area (European Commission, 2000d) and a stronger Community innovation policy (European Commission, 2003c). In this chapter we examine all three by reference to human investment (European Round Table of Industrialists, 2001; European Commission, 2003b; 2003d).

Common to these initiatives is a recognition that the countries of the EU will need substantially to raise their performance, as far as human investment and skills are concerned, if they are not to fall further behind the USA in particular. Thus, for example, the *Communication on Innovation Policy* (European Commission, 2003c), in drawing attention to the generally weak position of the EU relative to the US and Japan, highlights specialist skill shortages and, with an ageing population, the need for more vigorous lifelong training. At the same time, these EU policy documents recognise that it is not simply a matter of imitating the US experience: in particular, they express hopes for patterns of economic development which involve stronger social cohesion, not least by extending education and training opportunities in the new economy to the whole population (European Commission, 2003d).

Traditionally a major difference between the US and many EU countries has been the stronger development in Europe of vocational training. Not that this has followed a single pattern (Crouch et al, 1999; Estevez-Abe et al, 2001). The German model traditionally focused on firm and industry-specific skills, to be acquired before full entry into the labour market, within a well-defined skill hierarchy. In Scandinavia and France, the focus was on more general vocational skills within a less rigid hierarchy. The more rapid outdating of vocational skills entailed by the new economy poses a major challenge for these systems.

EU policy initiatives concerned with human investment give a central place to the new information technologies and the economic, social and educational changes with which they are associated. Education and training have a vital part to play in forging a knowledge-based economy which is socially cohesive: but education and training themselves face major change as a result of these same technologies. These EU initiatives refer for example to e-learning (European Commission, 2001d), lifelong learning (European Commission, 2000b; European Commission, 2003i) and the overall objectives of education and training systems in a global and knowledge-based economy (European Commission, 2001g; European Commission, 2003j; 2004f).

These initiatives involve a major change in the European policy landscape as compared with as little as ten years ago. At that stage education was a policy area into which the EU institutions made very limited incursions, even if their role in relation to vocational training was much stronger. Only with the turn of the century, and the recognition that the success of the European economy will depend on its reconfiguration as a knowledge-based economy, have policies for education and training, employment and innovation, been brought together as a coherent European priority, with the new information technologies at the centre.

This chapter investigates human investment by reference to the model of innovation and transformation we developed in Chapter 4, seeking to identify benchmarking indicators that might be used by policy makers at national and European level.

Stage 1: Preparation and invention

Organisations which provide education and training have a double involvement in the knowledge based economy. Like the enterprises which we studied in the previous chapter, they confront the technological and organisational challenges of the new economy: if they are to survive and prosper, they are obliged to rethink their whole *modus operandi*. This means taking stock of scarce resources, identifying leading-edge best practice and devising innovatory strategies. Secondly, however, the 'outputs' of their activities – skilled human beings – are a key resource for the innovation systems of all other organisations. How adequately education and training organisations meet the challenges of the new economy therefore has multiplier effects across the whole society. (Some of their other outputs – in terms of research and knowledge transfer – are obviously also of great importance for the knowledge-based economy: these were, however, addressed in the previous chapter, in the context of the resources which enterprises can draw down from the national innovation system).

In order to capture key elements of Stage 1, key indicators must therefore include the readiness for innovation on the part of education and training providers; and human capital supplies and skill gaps.

Readiness for educational innovation

What was said in Chapter 5, about the readiness for innovation of organisations generally, applies also of course to education and training providers. As we noted there the available indicators are rather crude: the same goes when they are applied to educational institutions (OECD, 2004e). Thus, for example, the various EU indicator sets introduced in Chapter 2 give central attention to the ICT equipment with which education and training providers are endowed, and their level of connectedness to the internet, but very little in relation to the *uses* to which these technologies are put.

In the light of Chapter 5, what is also of interest, however, is the extent to which individual education and training providers can expect to be major drivers of innovation. Most of them are arguably in the position of SMEs, able to adopt and develop technological and organisational innovations only if the national and European 'educational innovation systems' in which they are embedded offer appropriate support. Indicators which capture the key features of such education support systems, in terms which would then allow benchmarking between countries, are urgently needed: as yet however there would seem to be little available.

Human capital supplies and skill gaps

Human capital supplies were of interest in Chapter 5 as an input to innovation processes within enterprises. Skill gaps were of interest as a resource constraint on the rate at which enterprises could hope to innovate and develop. Here in contrast they are a market opportunity, by reference to which education and training institutions rethink their operations.

What new skills are required in the knowledge-based economy? What are the major skill deficits? What is the relationship of these skills to the competencies which are being conferred by the increasingly diverse education market on which people are drawing? What indicators of these skills can be used for national policy making in regard to human capital formation? These questions are addressed in a

Figure 6.1: Human resources in science and technology

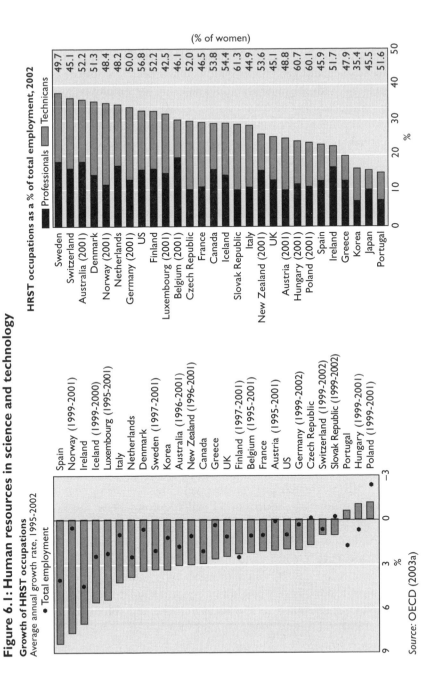

Growth of HRST occupations
Average annual growth rate, 1995-2002
● Total employment

HRST occupations as a % of total employment, 2002
■ Professionals ■ Technicians

(% of women)

Source: OECD (2003a)

variety of national and international reports over recent years, including for example *OECD Information Technology Outlook* (especially chapter 3) (OECD, 2002f).

The OECD and the EU publish HRST (Human Resources devoted to Science and Technology) indicators. These refer to the number of persons with a university education and/or employed as managers, professionals and technicians. Such data can on various assumptions (De Haan, 2003) be used to produce an estimate of the stock of human capital in a given country. What HRST indicators do not do, of course, is to display the relationship between the human resources available and those that are in demand.

In its *Action Plan for Skills and Mobility*, the European Commission (2002c) cited studies referring to skill deficits, which showed the number of unfilled job opportunities for people with IST and e-business skills (see also OECD, 2002f, pp 161-4). These drew in part upon data provided by the OECD, Eurobarometer and EITO, the European Information Technology Observatory. These forecasts suggested that while in some countries supply was starting to respond, the demand for professional ICT skills continued to grow and skill deficits persisted (European Commission, 2002f, para 2.2). In its report on the implementation of this Action Plan (European Commission, 2004g), the Commission finds that, with the European economy stagnant, major skill gaps have become less prominent: indeed, with the labour market signalling to young people that ICT-related jobs are less buoyant, applications for university ICT courses have actually fallen.

Nevertheless, forecasting methodologies remain insecure and robust indicators are lacking (European Commission, 2002g, pp 53-4). As the SIBIS research project observes, "there is an urgent need for a cross-country data source on IT skill requirements in the EU" (SIBIS, 2003b, p 42). The European e-Skills Forum, launched by the European Commission in March 2003, builds on the work of the ICT Skills Monitoring Group (European Commission, 2002g; European Commission, 2002f) and is charged with addressing these issues.[1] Its major report develops policy recommendations and proposals, including reference to the measurement and forecasting of e-skills demand and supply, a key element of its mandate. Such forecasting is however vitiated by slow progress in establishing internationally agreed definitions of ICT skills and skill levels and common guidelines for corresponding vocational training programmes (Petersen et al, 2004).

Three further important caveats must be entered, in regards to the substance of these forecasts and the statistical indicators on which

Figure 6.2: Occupations and skills in the information economy

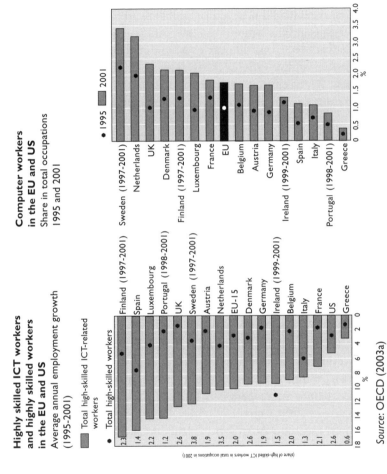

Highly skilled ICT workers and highly skilled workers in the EU and US

Average annual employment growth (1995-2001)

Computer workers in the EU and US

Share in total occupations 1995 and 2001

Source: OECD (2003a)

they are based. First, they are focused on the short term. The uncertain prospects for the new economy, especially at a time of general economic uncertainty, mean that beyond a year or two forecasts of ICT skill needs and deficits are little more than guesswork. It is not impossible that one of the novel features of the knowledge-based economy is that these skill needs are, and will remain, beyond any confident form of forecasting, because of the rapidity of technological change. This, if it were true, would pose major problems for any form of manpower forecasting and any national or European strategies of skill development. At the very least, skill 'life cycles' have shortened (SIBIS, 2003b, p 22). Nevertheless, the OECD study *ICT Skills and Employment* (Lopez-Bassols, 2002) endeavours to encourage a focus on the skills gaps of the future and to identify policy options for tackling them.

A variety of more radical views have been voiced (NESIS, 2002). One is that, whereas the skills which education aims to provide for the new economy tend to be defined by the business sector, the skills of tomorrow might better be predicted by looking, for example, at those which hackers are developing, as they seek to outwit the current ICT regime! Another is that the difficulties of forecasting the precise array of skills which the economy will need, and which the education system should presumably seek to provide, suggests that what may be more important is a range of meta-skills, including the ability to revise and transform systems: to such meta-skills a humanistic, liberal education may be at least as relevant as a training in specific ICT skills, geared to the technologies of today and yesterday.

A second caveat is that some of the recent shortages have been met by encouraging recruitment from other countries (Figure 6.3). However, few reliable data are available in regards to such mobility – or even for intra-EU movement. As for international mobility of highly skilled labour more generally, the OECD describes this as "widely uncharted statistical territory", preventing any "broad-based quantitative analysis" (see also Akerblom, 2001; OECD, 2002e, paras 22-3). As a contribution to improving this situation, the OECD convened a workshop in June 2002, concerned with the measurement of internationally mobile human resources, updating of the Canberra Manual (OECD, 1995) being one of the aims. Among the contributions to this workshop were attempts to pilot new indicators of the recruitment of young researchers from other countries (OECD, 2002c).[2] For the countries of the EU, the accession of the new member states, albeit with transition periods governing labour mobility, makes improved statistics on this front a political priority.[3]

Third, policy makers and employers are switching their attention

Figure 6.3: International mobility of human capital

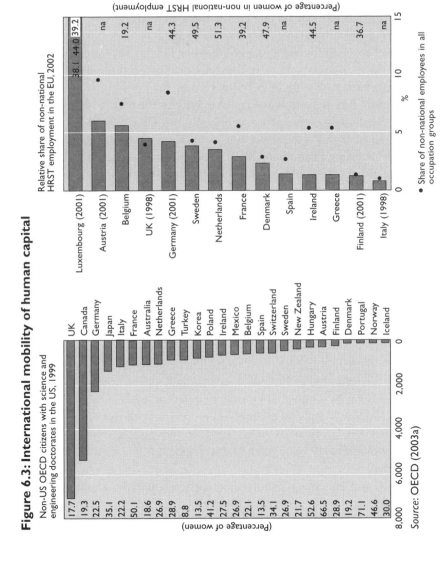

Non-US OECD citizens with science and engineering doctorates in the US, 1999

Relative share of non-national HRST employment in the EU, 2002

(Percentage of women in non-national HRST employment)

(Percentage of women)

• Share of non-national employees in all occupation groups

Source: OECD (2003a)

from quantitative to qualitative inadequacies in the skills supply. As seen in Chapter 5, the skills and experience for which employers are looking are not purely technical, but relate more to the application of technical skills in a business environment (NTO, 2001, para 4.2.1). Thus, even supposing that the difficulties of quantitative monitoring and forecasting can be overcome, indicators which take account of these qualitative factors must also be sought.

We have barely begun to address one of the key questions with which we started: what is the relationship of these skills to the competencies that are being conferred by the education and training system?[4] The education and training systems through which skills are provided are becoming increasingly diverse. They extend beyond the period of formal education: not just lifelong learning, but also 'life-wide' learning (Tuijnman, 2002). Little information is available about the skills acquired after people have left formal education (Pilat, 2002 p 12), although instruments such as the European Continuing Vocational Training Survey are beginning to remedy this gap. Finally, as Lopez-Bassols (2002) argues, if new skills for the new information society involve lifelong and life-wide learning, they also presuppose new forms of partnership among employers, education and training institutions, the public authorities and employees.

Stage 2: Application

Organisations which provide education and vocational training find themselves in a turbulent new world. The array of competencies which they are expected to provide is substantially different from those of a generation ago, most obviously in relation to ICT and its many applications. Many find themselves competing with rivals from beyond their own local areas, who exploit the new communications technologies to develop markets on a regional, national and even global scale.

The consequence is that many education and training organisations, in order to survive, are having to develop new 'products', new business processes and new organisational architectures as energetically as their industrial counterparts. Having said this, there are enormous variations in the extent of these pressures and opportunities: variations between countries and variations between sectors and levels of education. It is in higher education and in-work training that these pressures and turbulence are greatest and the urgency of developing new indicators is correspondingly acute. It is on these that much of our discussion will therefore concentrate.

Three sorts of innovation and transformation are underway:

- Education and training organisations are using the new ICTs to transform the learning environment. There is a widespread expectation that ICTs will be a major factor in creating more flexible, student-centred learning opportunities, although this cannot be taken for granted.
- In-work learning is also being transformed in response to the new information technologies: this is, moreover, linked to new strategies of human resource development, knowledge management and moves towards a 'learning organisation'.
- Leading education and training organisations are developing new strategic architectures, intended to secure their survival and prosperity within a highly turbulent new environment.

Indicators are needed as to how the new technologies for learning and teaching are being used and by whom (rates of involvement and utilisation by persons and organisations). Also needed are indicators of the extent to which, in the country or sector concerned, education and training organisations are putting together the appropriate mix of ICT investment, human skills, organisational change and entrepreneurship which together make for virtuous trajectories of dynamic innovation and transformation. What is also of interest to policy makers is the extent to which preparation and invention at Stage 1 are applied at Stage 2 and exploited at Stage 3, rather than petering out. These are in general indicators of intensity.

New learning environments

Among the indicators being used by the European Commission (see, for example, European Commission, 2000c) are indicators concerned with the linkage of educational institutions to the internet and training of teachers in ICT. Similar indicators are used by the OECD (OECD, 2000) and individual national governments (UK Cabinet Office, 2000, ch 4 provides a cross-national benchmarking survey). However, these indicators, while useful, are hardly sufficient as indicators of change in the environment for teaching and learning.

The OECD, through its Centre for Education Research and Innovation (CERI), has initiated a programme of work concerned with the impact of ICT on the quality of learning. Within this programme, Venezky and David (2002) bring together evaluations of a large number of case studies of ICT and organisational change in schools across the countries of the OECD. While their findings are detailed and complex, their key conclusions can be stated in relatively simple terms.

First, even those indicators which seek to capture the availability of these new technologies to educational institutions are of questionable utility. Indicators of PCs per pupil or per teacher can conceal very different patterns of utilisation, with no shared definitions of best practice yet available. Indicators of internet connection can be difficult to compare because bandwidth, firewall software and other features of communications software shape the utility of such connections. As Venezky and David comment: "So far we have no standard throughput measure for internet connectivity comparable to the benchmark programs that are employed for measuring CPU speed and memory access" (para 85).

Second, the introduction of ICT into schools does not by itself generate organisational and pedagogical change. The latter depends crucially upon the strategic choices made by the leaders of the institution or by particular champions of ICT-related innovation. It also depends on the cultures of educational institutions: their openness to change, the extent to which they punish mistakes and risk-taking (and hence discourage innovation), their support to staff development (Roberts et al, 2002; OECD, 2004a). (That these risks are very real is confirmed by CEDEFOP through its surveys of practitioners: CEDEFOP, 2002a, p 28). These factors are in turn shaped by national policies and resourcing regimes. The availability of ICT may be a necessary condition for such innovation but it is not sufficient. These conclusions from CERI are consistent with those emerging from the fourth and fifth Framework Programmes of the EU, addressing the socio-economic impact of e-learning (European Commission, 2003f, para 2.4). They are also consistent with the recommendations of the Commission's e-learning Industry Group (ELIG (eLearning Industry Group), undated, Section 2). Finally, of course, they are consistent with our assessment in the previous chapter of ICT adoption by enterprises.

The corollary is that indicators which refer to the ICT resources available in educational institutions and their connectedness to the internet may be poor predictors of educational innovation. Indicators are also needed of a variety of 'softer' factors, concerned with the purposes to which these technologies are put. A starting point may be the ICT competences of teachers: whether they can use the ICT technology and recognise the best of educational software. Increasingly, however, the search is for indicators of learning environments and institutional cultures in which student-centred learning can flourish.

It is commonly assumed that the introduction of ICT into educational environments will automatically facilitate student–centred learning and a movement away from the rote learning which is traditional in some educational system. Against this, Venezky and David note that ICT can be used to consolidate and reinforce these traditions, if this strategic choice is made by the educational leaders concerned.[5] Again, therefore, if the purpose of our statistical indicators is to measure not just the application of a new technology, but the extent to which this enables a student–centred, problem–solving, 'learning how to learn' pedagogy (which, all seem to agree, is required for a modern, dynamic, knowledge–based economy), the indicators currently in use are quite insufficient.

A variety of efforts are under way to address these inadequacies. Thus, for example, the DELOS project (Menon Network, 2003) provides an observatory on e-learning developments to accompany the e-learning Action Plan of the EU. The focus is on the range of changes in learning environments that the introduction of ICT has permitted. The DELOS indicators include reference to the quality of the learning environment, as judged by both teachers and learners. Nevertheless, indicators based simply upon the subjective assessments which these stakeholders offer are perhaps not enough; and for few of the DELOS indicators are statistical data currently collected on a systematic basis. Parallel work has been undertaken by the SIBIS research project, piloting indicators of learning environments in which student–centred learning can flourish: see SIBIS (2001). Nevertheless, as SIBIS notes, there would seem to be no existing data sources at international level on which such indicators could be based (SIBIS, 2001, para 8.2).

It is important to stress that it is not only the pedagogical and cultural strategies within individual schools that are significant: what also matters are the larger networks and cultures of the national educational innovation systems within which individual schools are embedded. The latest OECD assessment judges that, at least in regards to primary and secondary schooling, these have in general adopted the new modes of innovation of the knowledge-based economy much more slowly than have other sectors (OECD, 2004e). Nevertheless, this assessment remains at the level of qualitative generalisation and no indicators are offered that might be of interest here.

Finally, it is worth noting that to capture the qualitative changes in learning environments which these new technologies permit may only to a limited extent be possible using quantitative indicators. What may also be needed are qualitative accounts of good practice, tapping into the specificities of national context and the path dependencies these involve: 'benchlearning', as distinct from benchmarking (Room, 2003). To this we return in more general terms in Chapter 9.

The learning organisation

So far we have focused on formal educational provision. However, the vocational training provided at work is of growing importance for lifelong learning in a knowledge-based economy, and this also is being transformed by the new information technologies.

Training and skill development are not self-contained activities. As seen in Chapter 5, for any organisation aiming at dynamic innovation and transformation, it is essential to bring together its knowledge management, its development of human resources and entrepreneurship and its ICT investment, so that they are mutually reinforcing (OECD, 2003b, ch 3). This is central to the vision of the 'learning organisation' (Nyhan et al, 2003a; 2003b; 2004). It is also central to many of the policy documents emanating from the EU institutions, the OECD and national governments, concerned with the promotion of innovation, productivity and dynamic transformation within the new knowledge-based economy. With enterprises keen to have 'just-in-time learning' at their disposal, flexible forms of learning using new

Figure 6.4: Proportion of employees participating in CVT courses, EU, 1999 (%)

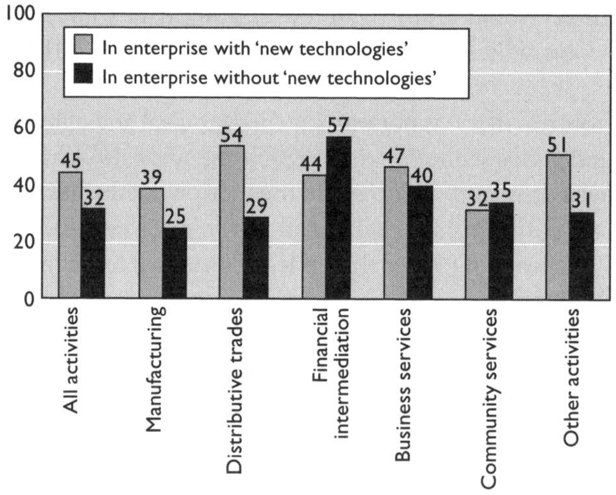

Source: European Commission (2003k)

information technologies are even more relevant here than in conventional education and training institutions (Roberts et al, 2002). However, this does not necessarily mean that these new learning technologies are energetically and systematically adopted: this depends on a range of contextual and institutional factors, enabling or blocking such take-up, and the national innovation systems within which enterprises are embedded (Attwell, 2003).

Nor does it necessarily follow that the interests of employees and enterprises coincide in some simple fashion. Organisational strategies and patterns of transformation may seek to make better use of employees' skills and potentialities, but this does not mean that workers' self-development is their central goal. Nor, however, can it be assumed that workers themselves are concerned first and foremost with self-development at work, as compared with extrinsic rewards, security and power. Just as new technologies introduced into teaching environments can be used for a variety of purposes, depending on the culture and organisational leadership of the schools in question, and may not lead automatically to student-centred learning, so also with the introduction of new technologies of information management within enterprises.

Many similar conceptual and methodological issues to those raised above in the case of formal education recur here. Thus, for example, Attwell, in his review for DG Education and Culture of e-learning and SMEs, stresses the decisive role of managers in shaping the ways in which ICT is used to support learning within SMEs (Attwell, 2003). A wide variety of modes of in-work training are possible: policy makers may need to intervene significantly in the national innovation systems concerned, if enterprises are to be encouraged along trajectories of dynamic innovation and transformation. This might, Attwell suggests, include support for regional learning networks, which would enable managers to address in-work learning not in isolation, but in the context of organisational change and the management of new technology (see similarly the discussion in the previous chapter of support for innovation by SMEs).

New indicator systems appropriate to these developments are only slowly being put in place. One example is the EU-wide enquiry into working conditions, regularly undertaken by the European Foundation for the Improvement of Living and Working Conditions (and most recently applied to the new accession states) (European Foundation for the Improvement of Living and Working Conditions, 2001). The indicators generated by these surveys cover a range of relevant issues – use of ICT, involvement in training, contribution to discussions of organisational change: they also break them down by gender and employment status, as well as country. Using these indicators, the European Foundation is able to highlight a number of trends and cross-sectional contrasts: for example, the higher levels of learning and training at work enjoyed by 'core workers' – males, higher grade workers – but the evidence also that some of these differentials are reducing, as atypical workers are given greater access to training. It is also evident that there are strong cross-national variations, with the Scandinavian countries, for example, well ahead in terms of inclusion within discussion of organisational change. These indicators thus provide a starting point at least in tracking the development of 'learning organisations' in a knowledge-based economy.

New strategic architectures

Education and training organisations – key providers of human investment – are faced with a turbulent and increasingly globalised educational economy. If they are to survive, they must develop new business strategies and new organisational architectures, as energetically as their industrial counterparts. It is on these developments that we now focus, with particular reference to post-compulsory education.

As seen earlier, the risks and opportunities with which the new economy presents education and training organisations are of perhaps three sorts. First, it generates new requirements for human capital and skills: these in turn drive the aspirations of those who seek post-compulsory education. Second, it offers new technologies for use in education, which these institutions are exploiting through novel organisational and market strategies. Third, the communications revolution means that exploitation of these technologies can be attempted across a global terrain. This globalisation is assisted by concurrent developments such as the political drive for open markets under the auspices of the WTO, including GATS (Knight, 2003; OECD, 2004f, section 1.5.2 and Annexes A and B): education and training systems no longer operate within protected local, regional and national domains.[6]

The process of globalisation means that education and training organisations are, to an increasing extent, working across frontiers. As they do so, they are liable to come into competition with each other and to challenge the national educational regimes of the countries they enter. However, it is not only from fellow universities that these threats are coming. With the emergence of a global mass market in post-compulsory education, traditional universities face competition from new private universities[7] and are also exposed to the growing threat from corporate universities (Taylor and Paton, 2002). The latter may lack the esteem of the traditional public university, but they can bring the entrepreneurial strengths of the corporate sector and its familiarity with operating in international mass markets. They also bring technological sophistication from the commercial world and are at the forefront of developing online learning. They have moreover the experience of providing employee training programmes, even if they are now venturing more widely to address the education and training needs of a larger public. They nevertheless face difficulties in delivering a mass online service which will satisfy consumers, both in its pedagogical richness and its credibility within the labour market at large. There is a high rate of failure and 'creative destruction' (Newman and Couturier, 2002; Naidoo and Jamieson, 2004, p 5).

Of course, higher education delivers not only a set of skills, but also credentials that confer status and allow the bearers in some degree to monopolise access to particular desirable segments of the occupational structure. What is more, this status depends in part on the brand and traditional reputation of the university concerned, and not just on the effectiveness of its marketing or even of its teaching. Brand loyalty rather than fitness for purpose play a part in securing domination over the higher education market: competition from lower status institutions and corporate universities, no matter how entrepreneurial their business strategies and agile their organisational architectures, is accordingly blunted. Nevertheless, as higher education institutions venture far from their domestic origins, where these brands and reputations were forged, they are less able to rely on such loyalties, and must face the competition from their corporate rivals on more equal terms (Room, 2000).

Faced with these threats, universities are becoming entrepreneurial, albeit at different speeds, depending in part on the different national educational regimes and innovation systems in which they are embedded and the agendas being developed by national governments (Currie and Newson, 1998).[8] In some cases governments provide universities with a secure, if not generous, resource base and its staff with the esteem reserved for public servants, expecting them then to serve the national community by undertaking social selection and transmitting a national culture.[9] Substantially different are those countries where the university is treated as a quasi-private enterprise, faced with an increasingly uncertain array of threats and opportunities, and with diminishing security as far as its resource base is concerned. In such an uncertain world, its survival requires it to identify and hone a set of core activities where it enjoys some comparative advantage and where through specialisation it can enjoy some economies of scale. It may also develop a range of alliances (national, regional, global) with institutions – including for-profit and corporate organisations – which have complementary strengths, which can extend its offering beyond its own areas of specialisation, and provide avenues through which it can move with agility into new areas of specialisation, when circumstances permit. To the extent that a given university can establish hegemony in such alliances, it can focus on high value-added activities, maintaining its own room for manoeuvre while leaving less lucrative or prestigious activities to its partners. These strategic choices and organisational configurations have significant parallels with those discussed in the previous chapter in relation to enterprises: see in particular the discussion of changing structures, processes and boundaries, drawing on the work of Pettigrew et al (2003).

In light of the above, we focus on two groups of questions, and consider possible indicators. First, upon what combinations of ICT investment, human skills, organisational change and entrepreneurship does dynamic innovation and transformation in this new educational economy depend? Over the last decade, there have been many experiments by public institutions and private corporations, using these new technologies to transform the education and training environment. Many have failed, including most recently the UK's attempt to develop an e-University supported by a wide range of British higher education institutions (OBHE, 2004b). The consensus that seems to be emerging is that multi-mode programmes, combining online and conventional learning in a variety of pedagogical styles ('blended learning'), are the most effective and sustainable. In the case of cross-border programmes, this probably requires strategic alliances with local agents (Ryan, 2002; Naidoo and Jamieson, 2004).

The Observatory on Borderless Higher Education has piloted a benchmarking tool which compares and scores the performance of individual universities in relation to IT infrastructure, staff training, online learning both on-campus and distance, and strategic overall management of these developments (OBHE, 2003b). In principle, such an instrument can capture at the level of the individual organisation the ways in which it brings together its ICT investment, human skills, organisational change and entrepreneurship, so that they are mutually reinforcing, in generating dynamic innovation and transformation. The Observatory has piloted this tool with 102 Commonwealth universities from seventeen countries, both developed and developing, and is currently reviewing its utility. From such a benchmarking tool, it might then in principle be possible to construct indicators, enabling policy makers to identify the intensity of such innovation and transformation within different countries of the EU. Are some countries seeing their education and training organisations attain leading edge positions internationally, rather than having their education and training systems shaped by others? How well placed are different EU countries to capture international mass markets in post-compulsory education?

Second, within this new economy of education and training, with its interrelated challenges of globalisation, marketisation and new information technologies, to what extent are corporate and public education and training organisations moving away from their traditional and somewhat protected niches and targeting the same markets, whether with a view to competing, or to opening new opportunities for joint action? Indicators of the growth of private and corporate universities have been rather limited (Levy, 2003). Among the regions for which they are available are the countries of central and eastern Europe, including many of the new member states of the EU: these (UNESCO) data are however limited to the numbers of such institutions based within the countries concerned and ignore cross-border provision by global players (http://www. cepes.ro).

The Observatory on Borderless Higher Education has developed a *Global Education Index,* referring to major for-profit global providers of post-compulsory education which are publicly traded (Garrett and Maclean, 2004). The index tracks the share price and financial results of fifty leading providers, selecting them by reference not only to the scale of their activities, but also the extent of their competition with, or service to, the non-profit higher education sector. The index shows that while the collapse of the dotcom boom during 2001-2 saw setbacks in the GEI, these have now been reversed, with US-based providers doing especially well. The index is also valuable in generating a range of related insights, for example into the overall numbers of publicly traded firms operating in this broad area world-wide (fewer than 100) and the pattern of acquisitions and failures.

The studies underlying the index also provide insights into the broad business models adopted by these corporate suppliers and their competitive and service relationships with non-profit higher education: in other words, the new organisational architectures (Garrett, 2004). Two key findings emerge. The first is that while direct competition between the two sectors is still rather limited, it is nevertheless growing substantially, especially in the field of IT training, something of particular interest for the new economy. The second is that a wide variety of cooperative relationships are also developing between institutions across the two sectors, involving the input of specialist services, franchising, etc (but leaving it sometimes unclear as to whose strategic interests are driving the collaboration). The work of the Observatory does not yet allow us to develop indicators of organisational architectures as specific as those brought forward in the previous chapter (see for example the indicators developed by the INNFORM project): such indicators when available would however be of considerable interest for European public policy makers.

Stage 3: Diffusion

Processes of innovation at the micro-level are transforming the whole education and training system. To conceptualise and measure these processes of diffusion and transformation is however no easy task. One approach is to measure the extent to which the technological and organisational innovations developed at Stage 2 have spread more generally. What is the extent of this diffusion? What are the barriers? Which groups are the last to be included? Indicators are readily available showing the quantitative diffusion of new technologies across the education and training system. These indicators do not, however, suffice (as previously discussed) as indicators of the extent to which learning environments have been transformed under the influence of these technologies, towards a student-centred, problem-solving pedagogy. Indicators which capture these latter developments, and their diffusion across the society in question, are poorly developed.

A second approach is to consider how, as innovations diffuse, this also leads to the wholesale reorganisation of social institutions and markets. This reorganisation can, indeed, be a major prize for the sponsor of a given innovation, if it means that institutions and markets are recalibrated around the sponsor's standards. This in turn underlines that diffusion involves a struggle for dominance, the victors of which will be in pole position for subsequent phases of innovation. At Stage 3 we are therefore concerned not only with the spread of a given innovation across the society concerned, and the inclusion of even the laggards, we are also interested in the patterns of dominance that are thus established by the leading edge performers. It is on these issues that the rest of this section focuses.

The social organisation of education and training is being transformed by three interrelated forces: globalisation, marketisation and the new educational technologies associated with ICT, including online learning. This means that consumers are less and less confined to opportunities offered within their own countries. This could undermine the role that educational institutions have traditionally played in transmitting a specific national political culture and supporting specific national policies of economic development. It could have profound implications for the educational infrastructures on which nation states have traditionally relied, involving heavy investments in physical plant. It also means that traditional indicators for forecasting national educational needs are thrown more and more into question (HEFCE (Higher Education Funding Council for England), 2000). To understand – and then to measure – this reorganisation is no easy task. However, for national and EU policy makers it is essential, given the enormity of the challenges to education and training policy that are posed by these interrelated changes.

Thus, for example, the development of online learning enables universities to offer programmes to larger numbers of students than could ever be accommodated as conventional students on their campuses and, additionally, to include students who because of other commitments and constraints could not in any case consider such a conventional route to educational credentials. If students are satisfied with the quality of such online learning (perhaps supported by local tutors), they may then prefer to study online at a high status university, rather than studying conventionally at a lower status institution. (With increasing rates of participation in higher education, there are signs of increasing differentiation of higher education institutions by status and reputation: this is a key element in student choice of institution: Room, 2000). The consequences for lower status institutions could be dire.

The development of a common European education space – in particular for higher education, under the Bologna process – may tend to accelerate these processes (OECD, 2004f, section 3.1.3).[10] Such a space may well be a precondition for achievement of the Lisbon goals: the EU Commission has stressed the importance of removing 'incompatibilities and incoherence' among twenty-five education and training systems, if "the largest single market in the world [is to] become ... the most competitive knowledge-based society" (European Commission, 2004a). It may also be helpful in establishing a framework within which diverse national educational provisions and qualifications can be compared. More significant, however, for our present purposes at least, it will promote convergence and remove barriers to transnational entrepreneurialism in higher education. This may provide European-based education providers with the large 'home market' they need in order to become world-beaters. However, it may also enable particular countries to attain a dominant position, leaving other countries to see their education and training systems shaped from outside.

Nationally as well as internationally, statistical indicator systems have been left behind by these new developments. The OECD has launched various studies concerned with international trade in educational services, including the effects of e-education, and the implications for statistical indicator systems (OECD, 2004f). A series of studies are also available from the Observatory on Borderless Higher Education (OBHE). What immediately emerges from these studies, however, is the paucity of the data available and the inappropriateness of traditional statistical indicators. These provide a poor basis for forecasting supply and demand, especially when judged against the scale of public investment in educational infrastructures.

Nevertheless, given that online education is only now beginning to transform the international educational environment, and that what works or does not work is still unclear, it would in any case have until recently been premature to define a new statistical framework. For example, it is as yet unclear how far students themselves will accept educational programmes that are delivered entirely online, and how far it will be necessary to complement these with local campuses or franchised tutors. It is also as yet unclear whether appropriate quality assurance frameworks will be established, sufficient to secure reputations for online programmes no less robust than those of conventional programmes. Finally, within the context of GATS, it is unclear how far and on what conditions governments will commit to international trade in educational services (Knight, 2003).

What indicators would be appropriate to capture these developments? Given the investments that EU governments are still making in conventional educational infrastructures, it is important to have indicators of the relative growth of online distance learning, as against conventional learning. Equally, to the extent that a single European – and indeed global – education and training market develops (and recognising that there may continue to be substantial institutional limitations on this), it is important to have indicators of 'spheres of influence' of different countries, institutions and educational regimes.

Stage 4: Outcomes

The outcomes of interest can, again, be selected by reference to the Lisbon Summit and its goal of a dynamic knowledge-based economy. Relevant indicators could refer to:

- the quality of the education and training that is offered (including consumer confidence and general credibility of qualifications);
- the consequences of the transformation of education and training for the performance of learners;
- changes in the stock of human capital, not only in aggregate terms, but in relation to the specific needs of the new economy;
- market share in global education;
- stability and sustainability of the new educational economy

These outcome indicators are then of critical relevance to the readiness of the society to respond to further waves of innovation.

Quality of education and training

The more that the citizen is seen as a consumer in a global education market place, the more important it is to assure the quality of the alternative educational opportunities that he or she faces, and the information that is disseminated about these opportunities. Already in the late 1990s, the Council of Europe (Recommendation R(97)1, February 1997) was registering its concerns, not least in regards to some of the educational provision which was being marketed in the EU accession countries (see also CEDEFOP, 2002b, p 28). The OECD has underlined the absence of an international framework of quality assurance and accreditation in higher education, at a time of growing international trade in educational services (Larsen et al, 2001, paras 59-62; OECD, 2004f, section 6.4). With similar concerns, in 2002 UNESCO established a Global Forum on Quality Assurance Accreditation (Middlehurst and Campbell, 2003). Meanwhile, a growing number of major education importers (China, South Africa, India, Malaysia) are establishing tighter systems of regulation and quality assurance of their own (OBHE, 2004d; OBHE, 2004g).

Indicators of the proportions of online and cross-border programmes meeting particular quality standards should be of interest to national and European policy makers. This would hardly be feasible at present, with quality assurance systems fragmented and a lack of internationally agreed standards: these are issues that will need political as much as technical resolution (OECD, 2004f, section 3.3.4). Nevertheless, it seems that progress is being made: the Commission has launched an e-learning standards programme (European Commission, 2002h; 2003f) and, in collaboration with the European University Association, the 'Quality Culture Project'.[11] Initiatives such as the DELOS project, discussed earlier, are developing indicators of the quality and effectiveness of e-learning (Menon Network, 2003). Further work is needed, both at a technical level and in terms of consensus building.

The performance of learners

The PISA study of the OECD is well known as a cross-national comparative instrument for tracking changes in levels of competency and skill in well-defined respects. Other international surveys of learner performance and competence include the International Adult Literacy Survey (IALS) and the new Adult Literacy and Life-skills Survey (ALL) (Tuijnman, 2002). The assessment of performance and competency is however fraught with methodological difficulties, particularly in relation to lifelong learning. The adult learning literature argues that the outcomes of learning for adults may be less easily defined and, if work-related, may be more difficult to measure. Rather than measuring specific skills, it may be more appropriate to use self-assessment by the learner or to measure changes in performance or work satisfaction by the employee in the workplace. This is reflected in recent national efforts to measure adult learning, such as the UK National Adult Learning Survey (2002) and the Finnish Adult Education Survey (2000). The SIBIS research project also employs methods of self-assessment, in the various new indicators of digital literacy that it tests (SIBIS, 2001 paras 8, 9.1; 2003a, paras 3.2 and 4.1) these seem to have proved robust.

Changes in the stock of human capital

Our appraisal of Stage 1 indicators already included reference to the stock of human capital, as a factor affecting readiness for innovation. The new technologies of human investment examined in Stages 2 and 3, and the accompanying changes in institutional arrangements and modes of delivery, will lead to changes in that stock, and the need for outcome indicators. Much of what was said earlier is relevant again here, including the reference to HRST indicators. In addition, indicators of investment in ICT education and training, and the numbers of graduates from such programmes, are of obvious interest.

The rapid changes in the array of skills required by the new economy mean, however, that many conventional measures of human capital, based upon years of formal schooling across different groups of the population (see for example (OECD, 2002f, p 158) are doubly inappropriate. Existing skills suffer more rapid and extensive processes

Figure 6.5: Human resources

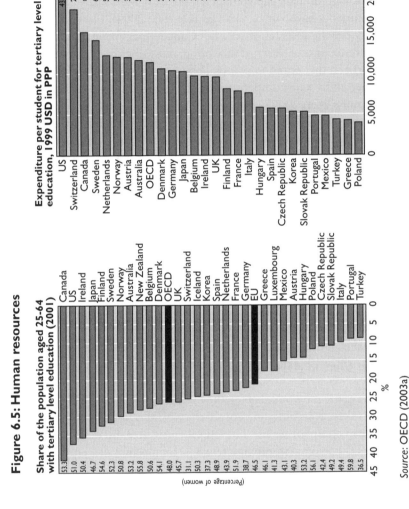

Share of the population aged 25-64 with tertiary level education (2001)

Expenditure per student for tertiary level education, 1999 USD in PPP

(Entry rates to university in 2001)

Source: OECD (2003a)

of enforced obsolescence, so that much of the existing stock of human capital needs must be 'written off' sooner, in a process of 'creative destruction' (see also our discussion of the skills required for 'digital literacy' in Chapter 7). Second, the shift to lifelong education, with greater emphasis on informal and in-work training, means that indicators based on years of formal education may become less relevant. Measures of human capital that could deal adequately with these developments have yet to emerge (Dencik, 2004). However, recent work under the auspices of Statistics Canada, measuring human capital by reference not to years of schooling, but rather to literacy scores – an approach that could in principle be extended to the measurement of other skills and competencies – has produced promising results (Coulombe et al, 2004).

There is one further consequence of developments in the new 'knowledge economy' which has implications for our measurement of human capital both as an outcome, and also as a stock which helps to determine the readiness for innovation of a given national economy. What matters for the dynamism of a modern economy, and its capacity to take advantage of the opportunities offered by new technologies, is not the stock of human capital per se; rather, it is the extent to which this human capital is brought together in agglomerations of appropriate managerial expertise, a highly skilled workforce, the exchange of tacit know-how, social capital and trust, well connected into the national and international innovation system and the communication technologies of the new economy (Porter, 1990; Dunning, 1993a; Held et al, 1999). Here too further work is needed.

Market share in global education

Here as in the previous chapter, the market share won by EU providers can be taken as an outcome consistent with the Lisbon goals, a sign of European competitiveness. The OECD estimates the value of trade in higher education as approximately $30 billion in 1999, equivalent to 3 per cent of total services trade in OECD countries (Larsen et al., 2001). However, these figures take into account only students studying abroad: they ignore revenues from cross-border e-learning and from the establishment of campuses and teaching facilities abroad. Nor do they include adult education and training, which appear to be growing rapidly and which could themselves be transformed through use of e-learning.[12] The OECD reckons that cross-border on-line learning – both education and training – will grow rapidly, albeit from a low base. The data that it is able to amass are however paltry: Larsen refers

Table 6.1: Percentage of foreign students enrolled in OECD countries by region, 1998 and 2001

Origin of students	1998 OECD countries in					2001 OECD countries in				
	Europe	EU	North America	Asia	Oceania	Europe	EU	North America	Asia	Oceania
Europe	79	71	17	1	2	81	72	15	1	2
South America	40	38	57	2	1	42	40	54	1	2
North America	39	37	56	2	3	38	36	55	2	6
Asia	28	27	49	11	12	29	28	47	11	12
Oceania	19	19	30	4	47	19	18	29	3	49
OECD countries	52	49	34	6	8	54	50	33	5	8

Note: The table shows that 79% of European foreign students in OECD countries in 1998 were studying in OECD member countries located in Europe, and 57% of foreign students from South America who were studying in OECD countries were studying in OECD member countries located in North America.

Source: OECD (2004f)

only to the numbers of Australian universities with offshore programmes and the numbers of foreign 'distance learning' students whom they have enrolled: OBHE confirms that Australia is the only major exporting nation officially to publish detailed data (Garrett and Verbik, 2003). Given that online borderless education is likely to grow, the share of this global trade taken by individual EU countries and the EU as a whole is of significance for future economic prosperity.

Much of the available literature focuses on the main English-speaking exporters – Australia, UK and US – and their efforts to tap into the expanding post-compulsory education market of Asia in particular (with other countries of the EU involved as exporters to a much more limited degree). However, even if these enormous Asian markets appear attractive targets for Western educational exports, this does not mean that within those markets Western exporters are becoming dominant. On the contrary, many Asian open universities are developing domestic and cross-border online post-compulsory education, on a very major scale, using their own in-house learning platforms and at a quality and cost that cannot be met by their western counterparts (Murphy et al, 2003). Where this is happening, future opportunities for Western exporters may be principally in specialist niche areas, for groups wanting English-language medium, or as partners to local institutions. Fears of 'content imperialism', to the detriment of indigenous cultural and economic priorities, may therefore have been exaggerated: the new patterns of dominance enforced through borderless education may be more complex, and more vigorously contested, than some have feared.[13]

Stability and sustainability of the new educational economy

Recent economic growth within the new knowledge-based economies of the OECD countries has been 'skill-biased', with a 'skill premium' (Acemoglu, 2001): the recruitment of highly-skilled knowledge workers has grown disproportionately, and their remuneration has risen much faster than employees in general (OECD, 2001, ch IV; US Department of Commerce, 2002a, chV). Pre-tax incomes are generally becoming more unequal: with social protection systems under pressure, it would seem unwise to expect some reversal of this trend (Forster, 2000). Meanwhile, with pressures on at least some elements of our education and training systems to move in a market-driven direction, the likelihood of compensatory measures, to give priority in lifelong learning to those who have least human capital, would seem unlikely (Room, 2002). The new economy could therefore breed increasing polarisation between those with and without knowledge-based skills. This is, not least, worrying from the standpoint of promoting economic growth: the aforementioned study by Coulombe, Tremblay and Marchand (2004) concludes that it is by targeting human investment on those workers operating at the lowest skill levels that the greatest contribution to economic growth can be achieved. (As Clayton (2004b) notes, this confirms the merits of including indicators of early school leaving in the Commission's Structural Performance Indicators (European Commission, 2000c), the backcloth to the more specific benchmarking exercises with which our discussion has been more obviously concerned).

Increasing polarisation – between those with and without knowledge-based skills – could also have consequences for social stability. Indicators of inequality of access and outcomes in relation to human investment, discussed in Chapter 7 below, could therefore also be taken as indicators of the risk of potential instability. So also could some of the indicators discussed at Stage 2 above, where we touched on differential access to lifelong learning opportunities for different groups of employees. While, therefore, it was in Chapter 3 and in a macroeconomic context that we considered macro-economic stability, it is worth noticing that developments here in human investment may also have knock-on consequences for the stability of the wider socio-economic order.

These effects are however by no means necessary consequences of the knowledge-based economy. Acemoglu (2002) has for example demonstrated that the 'skill-bias' of economic growth differs significantly across the different countries of the OECD, depending on the way in which the new technologies are applied and utilised. This may in turn be shaped by wider institutional factors: and be susceptible to policy interventions.

In relation to the countries of the developing world, many fears have been raised about the potentially detrimental effects of the intrusion of global education providers: including fears that they will come to dominate the most lucrative education markets, and that educational needs relating to broader social and economic capacity-building in the country concerned may be neglected. There are also fears that there may be a growing divide between high-quality, high-cost learning available to the elites of these countries and low-quality provision for others (Knight, 2003; Naidoo and Jamieson, 2004). Again, therefore, the patterns of educational development traced through preceding sections do not necessarily make for social and political stability and sustainability.

Finally, it seems entirely possible that the rapid pace of development of 'borderless education', along with the opening of large mass markets, especially in Asia, could produce a rather chaotic and unstable situation – in Durkheim's terminology, one of large-scale *anomie*. Efforts by national governments to control and manage these developments and to turn them to national advantage could themselves contribute to instability: see for example the succession of governments in south-east Asia proposing to turn themselves into the region's principal educational hub (OBHE, 2004a). The development of possible indicators of these latter sources of instability would be a worthwhile area of future work.

Conclusion

As in the previous chapter, we conclude by reviewing the indicators by reference to which policy makers might monitor, benchmark and steer the new educational economy.

In our discussion of education and training organisations, we saw that while there are plenty of indicators dealing with 'readiness', in terms of the spread of the new information technologies, some of the same limitations as were found in Chapter 5 in regards to knowledge management re-emerged here. Indicators of human capital supplies and skill gaps – a key point of orientation for education and training organisations – were also deficient: this constrained their scope for scanning and planning new and inventive responses to the challenges of the new educational economy.

In Chapter 4 we argued the need for indicators of the 'leading edge' of invention and application. These indicators would measure the significance within the country concerned of education and training providers which are generating and 'riding' new waves of innovation. In the present chapter we have sought indicators of this leading edge: the novel learning environments that are being forged using the new information technologies; the new strategic architectures with reference to which education and training providers are reconfiguring themselves; the penetration of traditional provision by new online learning; the spheres of influence within the global educational market that these innovations then confer. However, we have also noted that the wider diffusion of such innovations, across the education and training system as a whole, is likely to depend upon the support offered by the national and European 'educational innovation system' in which they are embedded: indicators of such support are underdeveloped.

Chapter 4 also argued for indicators which capture the intersections and 'complementarities' of the ICT investment, human skills, organisational change and entrepreneurship which together make for dynamic innovation and transformation in the new economy. In the present chapter we have pointed to some of the indicators that are being piloted by the Observatory on Borderless Higher Education, and that offer insights into these complementarities. More is needed.

Finally, Chapter 4 looked for indicators which could provide insights into the virtuous dynamics by which an enterprise, a region or a country can accelerate along the path to a knowledge-based economy, as well as providing early warning of less desirable trajectories. In the present chapter, we considered at Stage 3 how the wholesale reorganisation of education and training might enable leading edge performers to establish new patterns of dominance and put in question traditional educational infrastructures; at Stage 4 we pointed to the potential implications for the stability and sustainability of the new educational economy. We may have made only the first steps towards identifying suitable indicators: but at least we indicated how such work should go forward.

SEVEN

Social cohesion and inclusion

Introduction

Successive waves of technological innovation generate hopes of a 'social dividend' and an improved quality of life. The telegraph was welcomed in the 19th century because "technology supports a kinship of humanity" (Scientific American 1881, quoted in Fischer, 1992); some decades later the radio was welcomed, as "making us feel together, think together, live together" (Marvin, 1989). Similar hopes have been raised by the spread of ICT: personal computers, the internet and mobile phones could promote social inclusion, increasing educational and labour market opportunities and enriching social networks.

The "social dividend of technology" has been on the European policy agenda ever since Padraig Flynn, EU Commissioner for Employment and Social Affairs, established the High Level Group of Experts in May 1995 to examine the social changes associated with the Information Society (Steyaert, 2002). At the same time, policy makers have recognised that technology also produces risks and that innovation carries a fundamental ambiguity:

- "The Information Society promises new digital opportunities for the inclusion of socially disadvantaged people and less-favoured areas. Information and communication technologies have the potential to overcome traditional barriers to mobility and geographic distance, and to distribute more equally knowledge resources.
- On the other hand new risks of 'digital exclusion' need to be prevented. In a society increasingly dominated by the usage of information technologies across all sectors, internet access and digital literacy are a must for maintaining employability and adaptability, and for taking economic and social advantage of online contents and services." (European Commission, 2001c, p 4)

The *e*Europe initiative aims to ensure that the transition to an information society is socially inclusive, builds trust and strengthens social cohesion. This resonates with the Lisbon Strategy and the Nice European Council (December 2000), which identified e-inclusion as a key objective within efforts to combat poverty and social exclusion. In October 2001 the Council adopted a resolution on e-inclusion (European Commission, 2001c; European Council, 2001). More focused policy statements include the Ministerial Declaration of April 2003 *Towards an Inclusive Information Society in Europe* (European Council, 2003). A similar set of ambitions in relation to the social benefits of technology can be found in global policy forums, such as the United Nations Development Programme, whose Human Development Report of 2001 carried the subtitle *Making new technologies work for human development*. Global NGOs seem to share this vision, as illustrated by the digital opportunity channel of oneworld.net (http://www.digitalopportunity.org/).

At the same time, the importance given to social cohesion by the Lisbon Summit was more than a commitment to inclusion per se. It also recognised that the development of a knowledge-based economy in Europe's demographically challenged societies will require full utilisation of scarce human resources, drawing in all sections of the population. This chapter takes stock of the opportunities and barriers to social inclusion arising from the new technologies, the scope for policies to maximise participation, and the indicators by means of which such efforts might be benchmarked.

Stage 1: Preparation and invention

The new technologies generate new social risks. Those without access to ICT skills and knowledge may fall further behind as technology advances, with whole social groups becoming less able to participate in society. This may then make for growing income inequality, declining public support for policies supporting technological innovation and increased costs of social protection programmes (OECD, 2001). The new technologies also, however, generate new opportunities for hitherto disadvantaged individuals and households, regions and countries, to escape and participate in ways less restricted by their socio-economic status, geography or physical capabilities.

So far as countries are concerned, this optimism underpins the UNDP ambition quoted above. As for individuals and households, there are hopes that new ICT-based forms of communication, consumption, political participation and work will become available to all, with fewer obstacles related to conventional bases of inequality, such as gender, disability, geographical location or age. The Bangemann report (European Commission, 1994) saw this as being best achieved through the trickle-down effects of a free market approach; more recently this has been tempered with a more proactive approach towards social policies, primarily educational, which ameliorate risks of e-exclusion.

Access indicators

The inclusive (or exclusive) nature of the new economy is set initially by the degree to which citizens have access to the new technology. The differential access to new media has been labelled the 'digital divide', expressing concern about a social gap developing between the 'haves' and 'have nots'. There are at least three levels on which this divide may develop.

The first is global. A global information divide persists, even if the situation is changing rapidly, with China and India on the way to overtaking the US as the largest internet populations (Press et al, 2003). Recent work for UNESCO, to develop a digital divide index applicable across developing and developed countries, introduces the concept of 'Infostate': a combination of 'Info-density' (the stock of ICT capital and labour, including skills) and 'Info-use' (the uptake and consumption flows of ICTs, as well as intensity of use) (Sciadis, 2002). With the average Infostate score calibrated at 100, the most advanced countries have scores of over 200, the least developed less than 5. So also, the International Telecommunications Union, in its *World Telecommunication Development Report* (ITU, 2003), has developed a composite Digital Access Index, which ranges on a scale from 0 to 1 and incorporates indicators of infrastructure, affordability, knowledge, quality and use of ICTs (see Table 7.1).

A second level on which the digital divide is visible is between the member states of the European Union. Across the European Union, almost half of all households were connected to the internet by 2003. However, behind this lie major variations, with flash Eurobarometer surveys showing, on the one hand, a group of highly connected countries (Netherlands, Sweden and Denmark at two-thirds connection) and a group of poorly connected countries (Greece, Spain, Portugal and Italy). The same pattern can be found when looking at the connectedness of institutions – e.g. schools – rather than households. With the expansion of the EU in May 2004, these discrepancies have increased. Latvia takes over the position of Greece as the member state with the lowest e-readiness, while Estonia and the Czech republic have indicators that match the average of EU-15 (SIBIS, 2003c).

Third, a digital divide is evident within countries. There are significant regional disparities in the availability of broadband, internet access

Table 7.1: Digital Access Index Value, by access level, 2002

High access		Upper access		Middle access		Low access	
Sweden	0.85	Ireland	0.69	Belarus	0.49	Zimbabwe	0.29
Denmark	0.83	Cyprus	0.68	Lebanon	0.48	Honduras	0.29
Iceland	0.82	Estonia	0.67	Thailand	0.48	Syria	0.28
Korea (Rep.)	0.82	Spain	0.67	Romania	0.48	Papua New Guinea	0.26
Norway	0.79	Malta	0.67	Turkey	0.48	Vanuatu	0.24
Netherlands	0.79	Czech Republic	0.66	TFYR Macedonia	0.48	Pakistan	0.24
Hong Kong, China	0.79	Greece	0.66	Panama	0.47	Azerbaijan	0.24
Finland	0.79	Portugal	0.65	Venezuela	0.47	S.Tomé & Principe	0.23
Taiwan, China	0.79	United Arab	0.64	Belize	0.47	Tajikistan	0.21
Canada	0.78	Emirates		St.Vincent	0.46	Equatorial Guinea	0.20
United States	0.78	Macao, China	0.64	Bosnia	0.46	Kenya	0.19
United Kingdom	0.77	Hungary	0.63	Suriname	0.46	Nicaragua	0.19
Switzerland	0.76	Bahamas	0.62	South Africa	0.45	Lesotho	0.19
Singapore	0.75	St. Kitts and Nevis	0.60	Colombia	0.45	Nepal	0.19
Japan	0.75	Poland	0.59	Jordan	0.45	Bangladesh	0.18
Luxembourg	0.75	Slovak Republic	0.59	Serbia &	0.45	Yemen	0.18
Austria	0.75	Croatia	0.59	Montenegro		Togo	0.18
Germany	0.74	Bahrain 0.58		Saudi Arabia	0.44	Solomon Islands	0.17
Australia	0.74	Chile	0.58	Peru	0.44	Uganda	0.17
Belgium	0.74	Antigua & Barbuda	0.57	China	0.43	Zambia	0.17
New Zealand	0.72	Barbados	0.57	Fiji	0.43	Myanmar	0.17
Italy	0.72	Malaysia	0.57	Botswana	0.43	Congo	0.17
France	0.72	Lithuania	0.56	Iran (I.R.)	0.43	Cameroon	0.16
Slovenia	0.72	Qatar	0.55	Ukraine	0.43	Cambodia	0.16
Israel	0.70	Brunei Darussalam	0.55	Guyana	0.43	Lao P.D.R.	0.15
		Latvia	0.54	Philippines	0.43	Ghana	0.15
		Uruguay	0.54	Oman	0.43	Malawi	0.15
		Seychelles	0.54	Maldives	0.43	Tanzania	0.15
		Dominica	0.54	Libya	0.42	Haiti	0.15
		Argentina	0.53	Dominican Rep.	0.42	Nigeria	0.15
		Trinidad & Tobago	0.53	Tunisia	0.41	Djibouti	0.15
		Bulgaria	0.53	Ecuador	0.41	Rwanda	0.15
		Jamaica	0.53	Kazakhstan	0.41	Madagascar	0.15
		Costa Rica	0.52	Egypt	0.40	Mauritania	0.14
		St. Lucia	0.52	Cape Verde	0.39	Senegal	0.14
		Kuwait	0.51	Albania	0.39	Gambia	0.13
		Grenada	0.51	Paraguay	0.39	Bhutan	0.13
		Mauritius	0.50	Namibia	0.39	Sudan	0.13
		Russia	0.50	Guatemala	0.38	Comoros	0.13
		Mexico	0.50	El Salvador	0.38	Côte d'Ivoire	0.13
		Brazil	0.50	Palestine	0.38	Eritrea	0.13
				Sri Lanka	0.38	D.R. Congo	0.12
				Bolivia	0.38	Benin	0.12
				Cuba	0.38	Mozambique	0.12
				Samoa	0.37	Angola	0.11
				Algeria	0.37	Burundi	0.10
				Turkmenistan	0.37	Guinea	0.10
				Georgia	0.37	Sierra Leone	0.10
				Swaziland	0.37	Central African	0.10
				Moldova	0.37	Republic	
				Mongolia	0.35	Ethiopia	0.10
				Indonesia	0.34	Guinea-Bissau	0.10
				Gabon	0.34	Chad	0.10
				Morocco	0.33	Mali	0.09
				India	0.32	Burkina Faso	0.08
				Kyrgyzstan	0.32	Niger	0.04
				Uzbekistan	0.31		
				Vietnam	0.31		
				Armenia	0.30		

Source: ITU (2003)

costs and e-Government connections. At the household and individual level, internet access is differentiated in relation to household income, age, education, ethnicity, employment status and household type. However, gender appears no longer to be a significant divide and age has taken over from income as the strongest factor explaining variations. In the US the apparent narrowing of digital divides was celebrated in the Department of Commerce's *A Nation Online: How Americans are Expanding Their Use of the Internet* (US Department of Commerce, 2002b). Nevertheless, aggregated statistics of readiness can disguise widening gaps between the majority and the most excluded (Sciadas, 2002).

Although there are plenty of statistics on household internet access, this offers only a partial view of the readiness of citizens to participate

Figure 7.1: Age and education internet divides

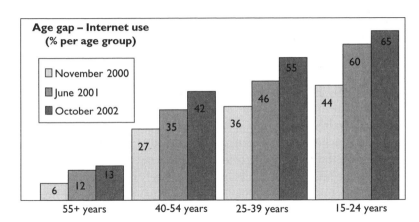

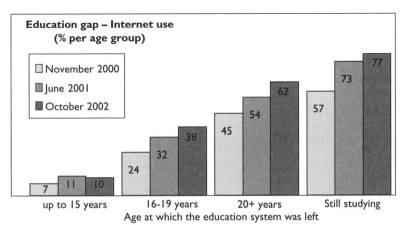

Source: European Commission (2003b)

Figure 7.2: Internet users by gender in the Member States (2002)

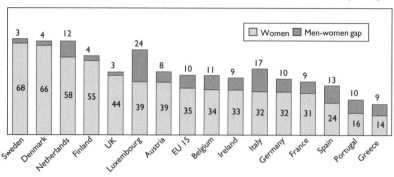

Source: European Commission (2003b)

in the new economy. Three refinements are needed. First, despite the dominance of the internet, access to other media must also be monitored: media such as mobile telephony and text messaging may become preferred technologies for accessing services and information (Nurmela and Ylitalo, 2003) and these may well have different diffusion patterns (Steyaert and Gould, 2005). Second, given the diversity of connections, having access to the internet needs to be differentiated, as between dial-in, DSL, cable or fibre-to-the-home. The emergence of such diversity is typical for later stages of a diffusion curve (Rogers, 2003) and may mean that exclusionary patterns are reinforced or reintroduced. Third, the location at which citizens or households access these media – home, work, public information access points – is likely to affect how they are used: internet use at work is likely to discourage the search for health-related information, while use at the local library is practically incompatible with file sharing (US Department of Commerce, 2002b).

Access to ICT resources depends partly on costs and is to this extent more difficult for those with limited financial resources. Costs of connectivity vary across member states by a factor of up to 3:1, depending on the characteristics of the connection (Teligen, 2002). Moreover, not all types of access are available everywhere: high speed internet access is concentrated in cities and economic 'hot spots' such as airports (Grimes, 2003), with less populated areas being marginalised (Prieger, 2003). Internal cross-subsidies to equalise connection costs were common in 'natural' monopolies such as the national telephone companies, but with the liberalisation of the European telecommunications market these are no longer feasible (Graham and Marvin, 1994; Markusen, 1999).

Patterns of access at different locations – home, library etc – may relate to each other in a cumulative or a corrective way. This is important for policy makers to know. Do schools in poor neighbourhoods with low household access have more internet connected PCs than schools in affluent neighbourhoods or fewer? If more, the inequalities in household access that we are observing may be less socially excluding than expected. There is however no empirical data supporting this hypothesis and several North-American studies supporting the cumulative disadvantage version (Kleiner and Farris, 2002).

A significant group of people with functional impairments are excluded from new media, as a result of their design. Thus, for example, the change from the MS-DOS operating system to the graphical user interface of Windows has made access to the technology problematic for people with visual impairments. Several elements of 'assistive technology' have been developed, but they often rely on the content provider implementing and respecting certain 'good design' rules. Equally, a majority of websites are 'designed to exclude' visitors with low literacy skills as a result of lengthy text, complex navigation and elaborate language. Finally, at least at the early stages of internet diffusion, the dominance of English content also excluded many people: as more non-English speaking countries come online, this dominance declines.

Digital literacy

Readiness to use the new technologies is limited also by digital literacy. Computer technology requires a new set of skills. Towards the end of the last chapter we referred to various instruments for measuring levels of informational competence: these tend however to be uni-dimensional and over-dependent on traditional literacy skills. A recent study from the Dutch technology assessment institute distinguishes three layers of information skills that are relevant for the emerging information society (Steyaert, 2000):

Instrumental skills: the ability to use technology, to handle the basic functionality of the hardware and/or software involved. These instrumental skills are similar to the notion of informacy and are targeted by initiatives such as the European Computer Driving Licence (http://www.ecdl.com/).

Structural skills: the ability to handle the new formats in which information is communicated. These involve, for example, the skill to look for information interactively or to make good use of the hyperlink structure of electronic information. These skills are relatively new and are induced by the technology.

Strategic skills: the ability to use information as a basis for decision-making. This level of strategic skill is not new: however, new technologies have provided the foundations for a society that is very information-intensive and where these strategic information skills are becoming of paramount importance.

Motivation

Finally, readiness is also related to people's motivation to gain access to, and make use of, new media. Motivation may be undermined by the lack of perceived benefits, avoidance of risks (loss of privacy, spam, pornography) and high costs. On the other hand, positive motivation is associated with the involvement which these technologies offer in virtual relationships and the 'social capital' the latter confer (Statistics Finland, 2004a).

In relation to both digital literacy and motivation to use the internet, *e*Europe 2005 is silent. Statistics Finland's communications capabilities index is an innovative and parsimonious approach to this (Statistics Finland, 2004a). SIBIS (2003a) has also developed indicators that are relevant to understanding motivation, such as perceptions of access possibilities and skill levels needed to use the internet. In particular, its composite measure of digital literacy, combining indicators of confidence in respect of various technical competences, broken down by age, gender and other independent variables, provides average and distributional measurements of progress by social groups in developing their readiness to use ICTs.

Stage 2: Application

Chapter 5 discussed the major changes that are underway in the organisational forms that enterprises adopt. These are intimately related to the application of the new ICTs: they are also, however, shaped by the specific cultural and institutional contexts in which they are embedded, along with managerial choices as to the organisational configurations that are appropriate. Within that same chapter we also noted the implications for those working within these organisations. In Chapter 6 we undertook a not dissimilar analysis in relation to organisations concerned with education and training.

These various organisations, public and private, are reshaping the world within which individuals, households and communities pursue their livelihood strategies. Global sources of innovation are mediated by these organisations, to create local patterns of opportunity and risk for these households and communities. Even more than the SMEs discussed in Chapter 5, individuals and households are change-takers rather than change-makers. They may do their best to pursue their livelihood strategies within the changing circumstances of the new economy, and in meeting these challenges they may, indeed, use the new information technologies in highly inventive ways. Nevertheless, their inventiveness consists largely in adapting to – and surviving within – a world that is being reshaped by these larger powers and principalities. Only as individuals and households come together, in well-organised communities and social movements, do they sometimes achieve the critical mass to lay hold on these larger processes. However, the capacity to do this is not distributed evenly across society.

We can analyse the inventive responses which individuals and households make to the new economy, as we already sought to do with enterprises and educational organisations, but we will need to take into account that they are in large measure change-takers. This modifies somewhat the conceptual model of innovation which we developed in Chapter 4 and which informed our discussion in Chapters 5 and 6. In particular, in this discussion of Stage 2, our principal focus will be upon the consequences for individuals and households of the technological and organisational innovations which enterprises and public services are developing and the new modes of social consumption and ways of life that these produce. At Stage 3 we then examine the conditions under which these 'SMEs' can absorb the innovations being spawned in the wider society.

The new ways of life that are thus wrought by enterprises and public services are commonly characterised in terms reminiscent of longstanding debates on the shift from *Gemeinschaft* to *Gesellschaft,* (accompanied by a similar range of positive and negative evaluations). Global supply chains managed by MNEs deliver an unprecedented variety of goods and services, many online, but sometimes at the cost of the disappearance of local shops (Lawrence, 2004). Teleworking and other forms of labour flexibility dissolve the straightforward location of employment at a single point in time and space. Local face-to-face community relations atrophy: new forms of virtual community appear as their substitutes. These new virtual networks are, however, 'weak' ties (Granovetter, 1973): they link the individual to a wide – often global – array of specialist expertise, but they cannot provide the generalised ties of traditional local communities. High-trust relationships are lost – as manifested for example in concerns about internet security – and new standards for quality and security control are required.

Such is the conventional wisdom as to the transformed modes of living that are becoming commonplace. In exploring successive stages of the innovation process, as experienced by individuals and households, we will seek in some degree to assess the plausibility of this narrative, consider the sorts of indicators that might capture its main features and identify the scope for policy interventions.

Enterprise and employment

Diffusion of new technology has often been associated with fears of job loss. The followers of John Ludd ('luddites') demolished new machines in early 19th-century Lancashire, fearing the loss of employment in the textile industry. In France, workers threw their wooden shoes ('sabots') into machinery and equally contributed to our vocabulary: 'sabotage'. Leading economists of the time such as David Ricardo expressed concerns about structural unemployment as a result of the deployment of machines (Ricardo, 1821).

The new enterprise architectures which we examined in Chapter 5 are transforming the labour market in several ways. First, technological change in the new economy seems to be skills-biased, calling for information literacy and knowledge workers (Esping-Andersen, 1999, ch 6; Esping-Andersen et al, 2002, ch 2). On the other hand, the new economy is also associated with the deskilling of labour and the 'degradation of work in the twentieth century' (Braverman, 1974), with large groups of (mostly immigrant) workers digging up streets to install cable infrastructure. These images relate respectively to the *upgrading* and *downgrading* hypotheses of labour market development in the new economy. Other hypotheses include duality, in which both low- and high-skilled labour is needed, but with the middle segment of the labour market diminishing. It is not altogether clear which account has greater validity in relation to the knowledge-based economy (Borghans and ter Weel, 2001).

Various of the afore-mentioned studies provide charts detailing the changing skill composition of the labour force, risks of unemployment and exposure to poverty (see for example Esping-Andersen, 1999). These are a valuable corrective to the sorts of indicator sets which have been central to the *e*Europe and related initiatives, which virtually ignore these aspects of the new economy. However, the relationship between labour market and work situations, the reconfiguration of enterprises and the changes associated with the new information technologies merits much more detailed exploration, as the prelude to elaborating appropriate aggregate policy indicators. It is moreover

Figure 7.3: Teleworkers by Member States (% workers reporting regular or occasional telework)

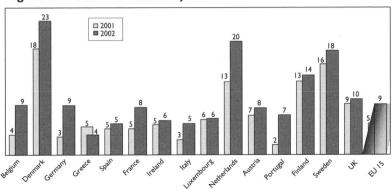

Source: European Commission (2003b)

likely that this exploration will need to take account of the varied national institutional contexts in which these changes are unfolding, rather than assuming a uniform development (Estevez-Abe et al, 2001).

Second, new technology revitalises the idea of telework (di Martino, 2001). In some cases this is mobile work, with people moving from city to city, from airport to airport, and working in lounges or temporary meeting places. In other cases, it translates to partial homework, with employment having an increased presence within the home environment. Again, two hypotheses compete and the evidence is inconclusive. The European High Level Group of Experts, considering information society issues for the European Commission, saw an increase in locally-bound social cohesion: "The information society provides the tools to increase distance working ... More employees working from home could result in increased social contacts within the neighbourhood and family, thus creating 'social networks' within communities" (High Level Group of Experts, 1996). Others are less sanguine: "The increases ... in telecommunications traffic suggest that whatever the amount of time people are spending at home, social life there is being sapped electronically" (Adams, 1999, p 119).

Education and training

In Chapter 6 we considered the effects of the new economy in reshaping the architecture of educational institutions and the environment for teaching and learning. Among the indicators that have been proposed, for tracking the effects of these changes on individuals and households, are those concerned with the connection of individuals and households to the internet, and the percentage having used the internet for training and educational purposes (see, for example, European Commission, 2002e). Similar indicators are used by the OECD (2000) and by individual national governments. Other indicators refer to the time employees spend on vocational ICT training (see Chapter 6).

However, much learning occurs not through organised programmes of education and training but informally, with the support of workmates, friends and peers (SIBIS, 2003b, para 4.1.1). Especially in times of rapid technological development, informal learning of this sort is likely to be particularly important, and must be regarded as a key element of lifelong learning, given the tendency of organised programmes to lag behind the pace of change (European Commission, 2001e). To develop indicators of such informal learning – whether in ICT skills, or in the wider array of new skills which the new economy has indirectly spawned – is a major challenge (Pilos, 2001; European Commission, 2002a; Tuijnman, 2002). As a first step, the SIBIS general population survey includes a variety of questions of lifelong learning and skill development (SIBIS, 2003a, para 9.2 Module C), aiming to uncover such factors as 'appreciation of the need for lifelong learning and regular updating of skills; recognition of the different types of cognitive skills and learning strategies that are required; working collaboratively in a variety of real and virtual learning environments' (SIBIS, 2001 para 7).

Figure 7.4: Participation in lifelong learning (% of 25-64 years age group)

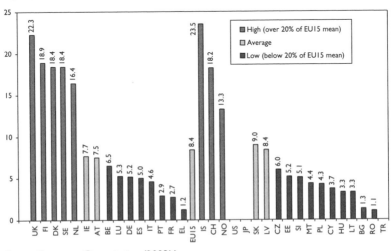

Source: European Commission (2003h)

Even such indicators would however be insufficient by themselves as indicators of the progressive transformation of household learning strategies. The latter depends not only on the transformation of the learning environment, and the more diverse array of learning opportunities that may develop, but also on the incentives which households perceive for investing in their human capital (see also the discussion of motivation above). This in turn will depend not only on public policies towards ICT and its incorporation into education and training systems, but also on policies determining on whom the costs of education and training – and the risks of such investment – should fall (European Commission, 2003i, Part C IV; European Commission, 2004d). Also crucial is the attitude of firms, and their readiness to invest in the human capital of their workers (Goldthorpe, 2000, chs 8-9; Estevez-Abe et al, 2001; OECD, 2001, p 63). In this latter regard, quite different national regimes are evident, even within the EU (Room, 2002). To identify suitable indicators of such regimes, and their significance for skill development and household human investment strategies in the new economy, would be a valuable avenue of future research, drawing upon some of the authorities just mentioned.

Public services and social welfare

The organisational architectures of public services are changing in response to the challenges of the new information technologies, along with pressures to reduce costs, reduce information inefficiencies and quicken response times. These changes may have an impact on social inclusion, in particular the delivery of services to harder-to-reach populations. In the case of welfare services, the changes involve a shift from 'Fordist' production of care towards individualised packages of care, the decentralisation of services to network organisations, the emergence of case management, and the increasing delivery by multiprofessional teams (Steyaert and Gould, 1999). In the health context Sermeus has described this as a shift "from functional departments to patient-focused care" (Sermeus, 2003). However, he also notes that in general the demonstrated links between organisational processes and improved service outcomes are weak.

Behind the rhetorical claims for 'needs-led' social care or 'patient-focused' health care, there are probably four domains critical to assessing whether these changes are making real differences (Hill and Zander, 2001). These are, first, the progression of individuals through pathways of care (protocols that map the processes and interventions that should optimally be provided by the service); clinical outcome measurements (mortality rates, readmission rates, changes in quality of life scores); financial outcomes (costs of the service) and service outcomes (quality of care evaluations by service users). Some of these dimensions could be quantified, such as the number of social agencies having a web-based presence and the depth of that presence (a simple website with address and opening hours, or provision of e-therapy). Nevertheless, it seems that as yet, none of these domains is represented in the indicator sets that are being used by official bodies, to track the development and application of the new technologies.

In relation to public services more generally, governments have made major efforts to develop e-government processes. There are a variety of indicators tracking this progress on a comparative basis, with some of these included in the *e*Europe 2005 benchmarks, including the number of public services available online. Other indicators that are being piloted include the proportion of public procurement processes that are carried out online and the percentage of public authorities using open source software (European Commission, 2005d). There are, however, no *e*Europe indicators that capture the extent to which these organisational changes improve the accessibility of services to people with special needs, something that is of obvious relevance to questions of e-inclusion.

*e*Europe 2005 does provide indicators of the percentage of individuals using the internet for interacting with the public authorities, broken down by purpose. However, there is no breakdown by demographic variables, to evaluate whether social groups such as older people or members of ethnic minorities are able to participate. There have been some efforts to augment this by surveys of citizens' perceptions of service accessibility, including electronic versus conventional means of data transfer, barriers to and advantages of online government services

Figure 7.5: Public services: availability online, 2004 (%)

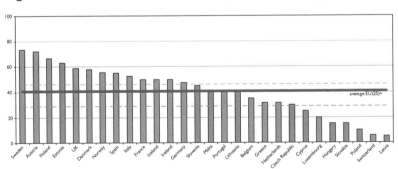

Source: European Commission (2005d)

and willingness to use online government services (SIBIS, 2003d). Again, however, these remain indicators of general attitudes and experience of online services, unable to illuminate whether there are particular groups who are being marginalized in the development of these services.

Stage 3: Diffusion

At Stage 2 our principal focus was on the new modes of social consumption and ways of life that result from the technological and organisational innovations which enterprises and public services are developing. We now examine how individuals and households are absorbing and responding to these changes and the positive and negative trade-offs involved.

Absorption and transformation

As with enterprises and public services, we are interested in the extent to which individuals and households are reorganising their livelihood strategies in light of these larger changes in society and economy. This means not only their usage of the individual technologies, services and opportunities furnished by the new knowledge-based economy, but the extent to which they reorganise their whole mode of consumption and production. We noticed in earlier chapters – in discussion of enterprises and education and training – that it is when a range of interrelated changes take place that dynamic transformations can occur. The same is to be expected here. What is also to be expected, however, as the backwash to such changes, is that there will be communities and households that experience progressive exclusion from this new knowledge-based economy and society.

As with earlier chapters, while indicators that capture individual elements of change are of some use, what is of potentially greatest interest will be indicators which capture these interrelated changes. We need indicators of interactive 'chain-linked' models of innovation, this time in household livelihood strategies, involving feedback loops and lifestyle transformation. As in previous chapters, however, we may need to be content with less than this, at least as far as currently available indicators are concerned.

Indicators of individual usage of the new information technologies provide a starting point. In principle they allow us to track not only the rates of usage of the new technologies, but also the activities that they displace and the range of activities which individual users can access, using these new technologies. The global Nielsen Netratings have expanded their internet tracking survey, to focus on 'active users' rather than the number of people having access. Active users are defined as people who actually go online in a given month.

A first element in the intensity of use is regularity or the number of internet sessions in a given time period. While some people use their internet connection on a daily basis, others activate it only once a week or less frequently. In recent years, there has been only a marginal increase in the regularity with which European citizens use the internet (Eurobarometer flash 135). Americans seem generally to have much more regular usage, their monthly number of internet sessions being around double that of Europeans (Nielsen/Netratings internet usage statistics). An explanation could be that in the US local telephone calls are free, with dial-in connections consequently unmetered (US Department of Commerce, 2002b). The regularity of usage seems to correlate with access patterns: it is lowest among groups with relatively low internet access (older people, those with less education). This suggests that the digital divide is probably wider than emerges from looking just at data on access.

A second major element in intensity of usage is the overall amount of time that citizens spend online. While the regularity increases only slowly, the number of hours that people are connected increases more substantially. What matters more, however, if we are to understand how lifestyles and livelihood strategies are being refashioned, is the way that this time is used and the activities that are being displaced. It is, for example, important to assess the claim that the new information technologies displace face-to-face relationships in the local community, undermining important elements of social cohesion thereby. Against this, there are an increasing number of studies indicating that it is time spent watching television that is sacrificed in order to spend more time on the internet (Mercer, 2004) (although caution is called for as these studies normally rely on time shifting as perceived by respondents, rather than time diary surveys).

Yet another aspect of intensity can be found in the very diversity of the applications that citizens use. The core applications of the internet are e-mail and web surfing, but others are developing and maturing rapidly. These include website hosting, chat, virtual offices (e.g. yahoogroups), online photo albums, instant messaging, file sharing, weblogs, etc. As people make use of more applications, there are incentives to improve their access to the technology still further and their level of readiness: in short, dynamic feedback loops. As this intensity of their engagement with the new economy grows, this is reflected in increased usage of bandwidth and increases in diskspace and the average size of e-mails. Internet Service Providers (ISPs) can monitor this in terms of the amount of traffic across their networks, the average size of e-mails and attachments, the percentage of subscribers making use of the web-hosting facilities and the average size of hosted websites. Indeed, the fact that in the digital world most activities are logged somewhere for technical or management reasons, opens opportunities to do secondary analysis on these data sets, similar to secondary analysis on administrative records (Hakim, 1982).

A further dimension of engagement with these new technologies is the extent to which people use new media applications in preference to traditional modes of accessing services and opportunities. When planning business and holiday trips, how many people still use traditional travel agencies, as compared with e-tourism? How many people rely on the traditional media (television, radio, newspapers) for news, how many on newspapers' websites or customised electronic newsletters? How far do people use the internet to gather information about their local community?

BISER has constructed indicators which estimate the proportion of the population who, during the 4 weeks/12 months prior to the survey, have participated in a range of internet-based activities, including online commerce (shopping and banking) and social networking (online discussion forums, posting messages in chat rooms, using email for private purposes). These surveys collect background variables on age, educational attainment and employment status, but omit other dimensions of e-inclusion such as disability and ethnicity (BISER, 2004d). BISER also has indicators of the spread of multilocational work, providing a regional assessment of these trends (BISER, 2004e).

Figure 7.6: Diversity of internet use

Percentage of EU workforce including unemployed

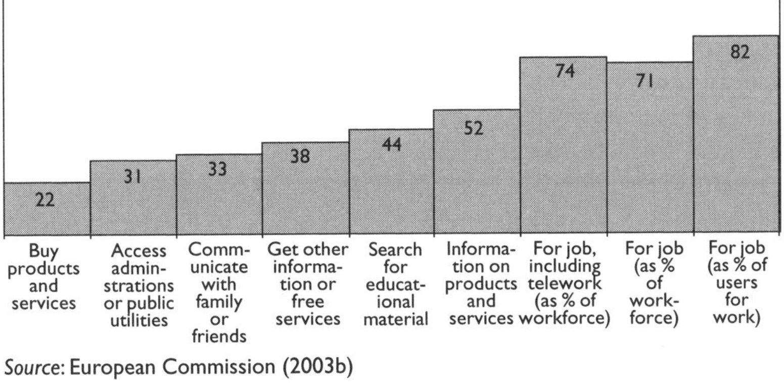

Buy products and services	Access administrations or public utilities	Communicate with family or friends	Get other information or free services	Search for educational material	Information on products and services	For job, including telework (as % of workforce)	For job (as % of workforce)	For job (as % of users for work)
22	31	33	38	44	52	74	71	82

Source: European Commission (2003b)

The internet has also revolutionised the availability of health information, rebalancing people's approach to medical services. According to a number of surveys, family doctors are increasingly seeing patients arriving at their consultation with a print-out of web pages (Vedder and Wachbroit, 2003). This development is not without problems, as it calls for a great deal of information literacy to scrutinise the information for relevance and quality. Given the lack of an editor or alternative quality control mechanism, the quality check is primarily the user's responsibility: "commonly used search engines do not discriminate between material provided by those with clinical expertise and those, for instance, advocating astral healing" (Hardey, 1999, p 823).

eEurope 2005 has a benchmark indicator of the percentage of the population using the internet to find health information for themselves or others. SIBIS augments this with indicators which illuminate more precisely the motivations for such searches, the outcomes, levels of confidence in the information provided, use of e-health and telemedicine systems and satisfaction with those systems (SIBIS, 2003d). All this provides an important profile of the general population's level of use and satisfaction with various aspects of e-health services, although it throws little light on digital divides, and whether health inequalities will be reduced or reinforced by such changes. BISER's work on health and care is an exception, in that its indicators of health information searches and internet communication with health professionals, based on its population survey, will map regional inequalities in e-health behaviour (BISER, 2004c).

Taken together, these indicators provide a glimpse, at least, of the extent to which individuals are reconfiguring their livelihood strategies in response to the new knowledge-based economy.

Infrastructures

Nevertheless, as already argued, households and individuals are in general change-takers. Their scope for reconfiguring their livelihood strategies in positive ways, to make use of the new technologies, depends on their access to these technologies, the training available and the networks of support on which they can draw for support and advice. There are obvious parallels with our discussion, in Chapter 5, of the factors which shape the absorption of innovations by SMEs.

As already seen at Stage 1 above, countries vary in the extent to which they have been able to roll out the technological infrastructure which is a precondition for e-inclusion. eEurope 2005 indicators include the percentage of households with broadband access, but this will not reveal the geographical distribution of access, and in particular the persistence of inequalities between rural and urban areas. The OECD has undertaken some cluster analysis of different national infrastructures for widening access (OECD, 2002f). English-speaking countries (US, Canada, Australia, UK) rely more on market mechanisms and have achieved high penetration. Lower penetration countries (Austria, Belgium, France, Italy, Switzerland) have concentrated more on access through schools and other public institutions.

Public Information Access Points are important in widening access: so is the increasing role of NGOs (Steyaert and Gould, 1999). Indicators of these community resources are included in some of the indicator sets that have been recently piloted, for example by the SIBIS project (SIBIS, 2003d). Further recent developments include the call for open source software and plans for deployment of wireless access points or fibre-to-the-home. Thus, for example, the city council of Amsterdam plans to deploy fibre-to-the-home in the whole city, arguing that this will bring many benefits, including better education for home- or hospital-bound sick children.

Exclusionary processes and contestation

Meanwhile, as households and communities are persuaded to use these new technologies, there are growing risks and costs of exclusion for those without access. The introduction of new media alongside traditional services can produce a diminishing customer base and the discontinuation of those traditional activities. Thus, for example, across Europe there have been a number of protests from associations of older people when railway stations introduced automatic ticket vending machines as a replacement for staffed service counters, or when banks insisted that their customers use automated teller machines to draw cash from their account. The discriminatory effects of these changes are reinforced when incentives are offered to customers using electronic services, such as the common practice of banks offering higher interest rates on internet accounts (Steyaert, 2004). This increasingly raises dilemmas for government about the political trade-offs that might have to be made between the costs of delivering 'trailing edge' services and the marginalisation of their users, e.g. in the UK whether compensation needs to be made to users of analogue TV if a complete switch to digital broadcasting is to be completed by 2010 (Wells, 2004).

With many of the new technologies that are emerging accessible only to those who are already well equipped in terms of ICT, these gaps between social groups can be cumulatively reinforced. Even if some of the more routine information technologies gradually diffuse throughout the entire society, the short innovation cycles for new technologies may mean that the technology gap between population leaders and laggards grows ever greater (European Commission, 2005c, Part A).

Stage 4: Outcomes

This chapter is concerned with the consequences of the new knowledge-based economy for social cohesion and social inclusion. These are outcomes which can be considered as desirable in themselves and as essential elements therefore of the 'social dividend' which new technologies should be expected to produce. However, as noted already, the preservation and promotion of social cohesion and social inclusion have a wider significance for the Lisbon strategy of the EU. The move to a new knowledge-based economy is expected to involve substantial economic and social disruption, under the impact of new modes of production and consumption: a new socio-political settlement will need to be negotiated, challenging some established interests and provoking a range of new social movements. EU policy makers are anxious to maintain social peace and win public assent for these transformations. At the same time, the commitment to social inclusion recognises that the development of a knowledge-based economy in Europe's demographically challenged societies will require full utilisation of scarce human resources, drawing in all sections of the population.

As we noted at the end of Chapter 3, the new economy is likely to have major consequences for the distribution of incomes and life chances. Indeed, as we saw in Chapter 6, recent economic growth in the new knowledge-based economies of the OECD countries has been 'skill-biased', with a 'skill premium': the new economy could therefore breed increasing polarisation between those with and without knowledge-based skills. The preceding pages of the present chapter point to some of the additional lines of division that may develop around the new technologies and their social applications. Whether these divisions are expressed in terms of class, gender and generational conflict, or in terms of Durkheimian *anomie*, they represent potential sources of instability, and ones which it cannot be assumed will quickly dampen down.

Social cohesion

One thing seems clear: social relations and patterns of cohesion are changing. As we noted earlier in this chapter, one common view is that local face-to-face community relations are atrophying, new forms of virtual community appearing as their substitutes. These 'weak ties' link the individual to a wide array of specialist expertise, but they cannot provide the generalised ties of traditional local communities. High-trust relationships are lost and new procedures for ensuring quality and security of service are required. It is with reference to these fears that we seek indicators of social cohesion in the society that is emerging: in particular, with reference to social capital and civic engagement.

Social capital

Concern is commonly expressed about the decline of social capital. Putnam, for example, has pointed to the ambiguity of the effects of ICTs: the availability of virtual relationships could reinforce social isolation rather than connectedness (Putnam, 2000). More recently however he has provided descriptions of situations in which it can enhance social capital (Putnam and Feldstein, 2003).

How does such concern relate to the emergence of new media and the new economy? While the communication network expands, social networks seem to shrink. This is the paradox that emerges from juxtaposing the two developments: how can more communication result in less social contact? Is social capital under pressure from the increasing use of new media, or is it the other way round: do we have

Figure 7.7: Effects by the internet on human and social capital (% EU internet users) (2002)

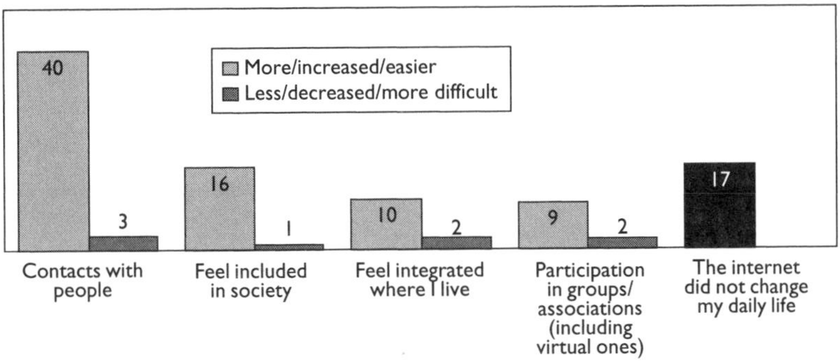

Source: European Commission (2003b)

more intensive information exchanges through these new media so as to escape our socially impoverished world?

In the early days of the internet, wild predictions were made about its future. Authors such as Howard Rheingold elaborated optimistic scenarios about local and regional virtual communities based on shared interest, such as his 'the Well' (Rheingold, 1993) and digital villages or neighbourhoods like the famous Blacksburg Electronic Village at www.bev.net (Cohill and Kavanaugh, 1997). Others voiced their concern about the effects of internet usage on social networks. These utopian and dystopian visions have however now largely been superseded by studies based on empirical surveys (Katz and Aspden, 1997; Kraut et al, 1998; Franzen, 2000; Rainie, 2000; Katz and Rice, 2002; Kraut et al, 2002; Nie and Hillygus, 2002a; Cole, 2003). These suggest that what matters is the status and strength of social networks prior to the development of the internet, as well as the place and time of usage.

It may also be useful to identify time displacement effects: how far time spent online detracts from those daily activities which might be said to maintain and build social capital. Such empirical data as are available confirm that time for friends, family and other social contacts does indeed suffer. So does time devoted to television and reading, according to both Eurobarometer (see Table 7.2) and time diary surveys (Breedveld and van den Broek, 2001; Nie and Hillygus, 2002a; Nie and Hillygus, 2002b).

Table 7.2: Time use of the internet

Did use of internet result in less time for ...?
EU 15 countries, population of 15 years and older, in % who agree with the statement

	Television	Books	Newspapers	Radio	Friends	Family	Sport	n
Population 15+	6	4	3	3	2	2	2	15,900
Population with internet access at home	34	22	16	14	11	13	13	2,917

Source: Eurobarometer 53 (April-May 2000)

Civic engagement

Concern is also commonly expressed about the declining level of civic engagement and the detachment of citizens from society. The new information technologies are then hailed as enabling a recovery of such engagement through teledemocracy, cyberdemocracy and e-democracy. This is related to – but must be distinguished from – the interest in e-government, where the main focus is on the quality of government services to the citizen. Within the e-government debate, the citizen is a consumer of services, not an active participant.

E-democracy and related concepts see the new information technologies as enabling citizens to become progressively more active: starting with information about what is happening, then moving to setting the policy agenda, political debate, consultation and decisions. Websites such as www.faxyourmp.com help citizens in voicing their opinions to their Member of Parliament, while www.mcspotlight.org supporters protest against the McDonald food chain. Digital debates are underway everywhere.

Two questions can be posed. First, does e-engagement improve its quality and effectiveness? This is related to the availability of technology and information, but also to digital literacy and authentication (e.g. e-voting). Secondly, there is the question of whether e-democracy tends to equalise the level of such engagement across the society. There is some evidence that these new technologies offer a new forum for those social groups who were already active.

Some likely trends may be discerned from a recent US survey conducted by Pew Internet, *How Americans Get in Touch With Government* (Pew, 2004). This found that the two thirds of US citizens with internet access are three times as likely as non-internet users to get in touch with government. However, the survey also found that the more complex or urgent an issue, the more likely citizens are to prefer telephone or face-to-face contact with officials. Groups at risk of e-exclusion – for example, people with disabilities – are particularly concerned to retain non-digital interaction with government.

Social inclusion

We now take stock of the extent to which the new technologies bring opportunities and barriers to social inclusion, the scope for policies to maximise participation and the indicators by means of which such efforts might be benchmarked.

Indicators of social exclusion and inclusion have been a significant part of the Lisbon benchmarking process. During the latter part of 2001, under the Belgian Presidency, various working groups and expert reports contributed to an agreed portfolio of indicators. Its most prominent feature was the specification of ten primary, and eight secondary indicators, all concerned with population outcomes, in terms such as low income, unemployment and ill health (Social Protection Committee, 2001; Atkinson et al, 2002). These indicators, slightly modified, have then been used in the second round of national action plans (European Council, 2004, section 10).

These are indicators of outcomes: outcomes at the level of individuals and households. Member states are expected to use and report these indicators on a national basis. The Joint Reports on Social Inclusion produced by the European Commission and Council (European Council, 2002; 2004) present the performance of different member states by reference to these indicators, albeit acknowledging the non-comparable aspects of different national situations and the difficulties in drawing comparisons. The same indicators were also used in reports relating to the accession countries (European Commission, 2004h). However, none of these indicators relates specifically to the new information technologies. The challenge is to develop indicators of social exclusion which do.

In earlier conceptual work on social inclusion, Room has pointed out that the shift in policy and research debate from poverty to social inclusion involved several key elements (Room, 1999):

• it reaffirmed the importance of adopting a *multi-dimensional* notion of inadequate living conditions;
• it recognised that people's living conditions depended not just on their personal and household resources but also on the material and cultural *collective* resources to which they had access, for example within their local and occupational communities;
• it focused attention on the *relational* as much as the distributional dimensions of stratification, recognising that relationships are themselves a component of human well-being, and that their breakdown or absence can therefore be a deprivation (see also, for example, Paugam, 1995; 1996);
• it acknowledged that much existing research involved a 'snapshot' of the poor at a given moment of time: what however was needed was to track the changes in the population at risk of deprivation between one time period, and the *dynamic processes and trajectories* involved (see also Leisering and Walker, 1998; Goodin et al, 1999).

Taking these elements as our point of departure, we can consider how the knowledge society and the widespread application of ICT involve a reconfiguration of the associated risks of social exclusion.

Multidimensional disadvantage

Access to the new information technologies is a resource whose absence can, on the one hand, constitute an additional dimension of deprivation, but whose possession may, on the other hand, serve to compensate for, and override, other deprivations (DiMaggio et al, 2004). In this chapter we have traced the changing lines of the digital divide as these new technologies diffuse: initially they reflect gender, income, education, but as diffusion progresses and a larger proportion of the population gains access to the innovative media, age becomes the predominant fault line.

As we have seen, however, the digital divide is more complicated than simple access: it also involves digital literacy and the skills to cope effectively in the emerging information society. These skills are assets whose absence is a further line of multidimensional deprivation. The various indicators of access and skills that were discussed at Stage 1, in the context of readiness for innovation, can also therefore stand as indicators of advantage and disadvantage: resources whose possession shapes economic and social participation by an individual or a community. Indicators of access are commonplace, as we saw earlier; indicators of digital literacy skills are still being developed.

Collective as well as individual resources

Access to the new information technologies – and to the skills which are required in order to make effective use of them – is a matter not just of personal and household resources but also of the collective IT-related resources on which people can draw, within their local and occupational communities. This has been evident at various points above. We noted, for example, that the location at which people access the new information technologies – home, work, public information access points – is likely to affect how they are used. We also saw in the previous chapter that access to IT resources in the workplace tends to be differentiated according to occupational status but also that this varies very much between countries and would seem therefore to be susceptible in principle to intervention (European Foundation for the Improvement of Living and Working Conditions, 2001). Indicators of access such as those used by the European Foundation give insight into the IT resources embedded within such occupational communities.

We have also noticed the importance of different national arrangements for rolling out technological infrastructures and for establishing thereby the collective assets around which individuals can then build their own IT strategies. This deployment may impact differentially on different communities: in many countries there has been concern about rural areas having less access to innovative network services such as broadband (although it is also necessary to take account of wireless networks and the availability for example of GPRS and UMTS services). To be effective, investment in community technology infrastructures must also, of course, take account of local institutional and cultural contexts (European Commission, 2005c, Part C).

Relational as well as distributional aspects of stratification

The new information technologies can lead to a reconfiguration of social relationships and forms of community, key constituents of human well-being. Thus, for example, earlier in this section we examined the ways that social capital and civic engagement are being refashioned, as people make use of the new information technologies, and some of the ways in which this might be measured. We have also referred to the transformation of the world of work, education and public services, and the changes in social relationships these involve, as witnessed for example in indicators of teleworking, lifelong and informal learning, new styles of social care management.

Dynamic processes and trajectories

The knowledge society involves socio-economic transformations which can send individuals, households and communities along new trajectories, positive or negative, in what may be an increasingly dynamic and unstable world, leaving public policies lagging behind. Thus, for example, while the new information and communication technologies may enable new virtual agglomerations of innovative expertise to be established, generating new economic dynamism and livelihoods where none previously existed, they also permit the accelerated outsourcing of jobs to other parts of the global economy, threatening employment and livelihoods and the degradation of the communities that depend on them. These are major themes of the foregoing chapters, on which our present discussion of cohesion and exclusion has been able to build.

Within the present chapter, we have pointed to the ways in which individuals are reconfiguring their whole mode of consumption and production – their livelihood strategies – in response to the new knowledge-based economy. We have suggested how these interrelated changes and lifestyle transformation might be captured and measured: for example, in terms of the changes in time use, the displacement of activities, the changes in face-to-face relationships. As people make use of more applications, there are incentives to improve their access to the technology still further and their level of readiness: in short, dynamic feedback loops. We have, no less, pointed to the accelerating risks and costs of exclusion for those without access to these technologies, as traditional services lose viability and are withdrawn. The declining availability of such services, or their greater expense, serves as an indicator of the progressive marginalisation of their users.

Conclusion

We end this chapter as we did its two predecessors: drawing together our broad conclusions as to the indicators that policy makers need, in order to monitor and benchmark patterns of social cohesion and inclusion in the new economy.

As we have seen, there are plenty of indicators dealing with access of individuals and households to the new information technologies. These are commonly broken down by various population categories – age, gender, etc – and trace the changing lines of the 'digital divide'. However, the changing gradients of these divides have not so far been captured in the main EU data sets, as they have in some official US reports. In particular, the US population bureau *Falling through the Net/Nation Online* surveys provide Gini coefficients, showing inequalities in ICT usage by reference to various demographic variables. Indicators of this sort can be treated as referring to 'readiness' for innovation. However, our discussion of Stage 1 also referred to some equally crucial additional aspects of readiness: digital literacy and motivation. Indicators for these elements are not yet well-established but some, as we saw, have been piloted.

Our discussion of Stage 2 focused on the new modes of consumption brought into being by the new knowledge economy, to which individuals and households are obliged as change-takers to adapt. Indicators of these changes are significant points of reference for policy makers, seeking to track the context in which households set about reconfiguring their livelihood strategies. They are also important if policy makers are to be able to identify the institutional supports which may be needed to enable households to take benefit from these new opportunities.

In Chapter 4 we argued for indicators of the 'leading edge' of innovation. We also argued for indicators which capture the intersections and 'complementarities' of the ICT investment, human skills, organisational change and entrepreneurship which together make for dynamic innovation and transformation in the new economy. For individuals and households, even if they are in considerable measure change-takers, we have traced their progressive adoption of the new technologies and their incorporation of the new modes of consumption into their livelihood strategies. We have moreover – most obviously at Stage 3 – pointed to the sorts of indicator on usage that can be employed to track these changes: the growing diversity of applications, the growing range of services, the dynamic feedback loops – 'the increasing returns' which users experience and which lock them into these new modes of living. We have also, however, pointed to negative processes of cumulative lock-out and exclusion that accompany these changes for some groups of the population and the indicators that can capture them.

EIGHT

Models and measurement

Introduction

In this study we have been concerned with the processes of dynamic change and innovation that seem to characterise the new knowledge-based economy. Chapter 4 developed a conceptual model of the innovation process: the subsequent three chapters applied this model to enterprises, education and training, social cohesion and inclusion.

The conceptual model broke down the innovation process into four stages. We used a taxonomy of *readiness*, *intensity*, *impact* and *outcome* indicators, corresponding to these four stages, with different categories of indicators being assigned to different stages of the innovation process. This taxonomy was by no means original. However, like other authors before us, we were then able to look for suitable indicators of readiness, intensity, impact and outcome, paying particular attention to those indicators that are being used by official bodies for tracking the new knowledge-based economy. Those that are being used by the European Union, as part of the Lisbon benchmarking processes, have been of special interest.

In this chapter we take stock of these indicator sets and their adequacy in light of our analysis. It is, however, first necessary to address two difficulties that we have encountered in the course of our investigation, concerned respectively with modelling and measurement.

Models

At first glance at least, the conceptual model of Chapter 4 was a linear model, with innovations proceeding through four stages. In our discussion of the model in that chapter, we took a more nuanced approach: technological and organisation innovation interact; streams of innovation cross-fertilise each other; there are feed-back effects from later stages to earlier; innovations can move along different trajectories, depending upon the national institutional settings in which they are embedded.

As we also stressed in Chapter 4, it would be wrong to imagine that the movement through these four stages is a simple process of technological competition, in which those inventions that are most fit for purpose will necessarily triumph. Hegemonic domination and creative destruction are also involved, as successive waves of innovation reinforce the position of those first able to ride them. This also, however, means that challenges, should they develop, will take the form not of seeking to imitate and undercut existing technologies but of technological (and maybe organisational) innovations that are on a quite different terrain. Many will fail, but those that do not may be able to outflank prevailing patterns of domination (Kelly, 1999, paras 3, 9).

In the subsequent three chapters, we have sought to apply these perspectives, in our search for suitable indicators of the innovation process. As we have seen, many of the indicators in general use, for tracking the development of the knowledge-based economy, refer to the spread of a given innovation across the population in question. These are useful in summarising 'readiness' for innovation: they also capture aspects of diffusion or impact: the extent to which a given innovation has spread to even the most 'backward' regions of the population. However, we have also pointed to the need for indicators of the 'leading edge', capturing the way in which enterprises, public services and maybe whole nations are able to capitalise on one wave of innovation in order better to exploit the next wave, thereby remaining at the forefront of successive waves of change. In the case of enterprises, we were able to build upon some of the European Innovation Scoreboard indicators of innovation intensity. In Chapter 6 we pointed to indicators which are being developed of novel learning environments using the new information technologies; new strategic architectures for education and training providers; the penetration of traditional provision by new online learning; the spheres of influence within the global educational market that these innovations then confer. In Chapter 7 we extended this to households, seeking indicators of their progressive adoption of new technologies and new modes of consumption: the growing diversity of applications, the growing range of services, the dynamic feedback loops – 'the increasing returns' – which users experience and which lock them into these new modes of living. At the same time, however, we also pointed to negative processes of cumulative lock-out and exclusion that accompany these changes for some groups of the population and sought indicators that could capture these exclusionary processes.

What has also become clear is that this 'leading edge' of innovation typically involves the integration of a range of resources, capabilities and organisational frameworks. This integration needs moreover to be accomplished within a setting that allows continuous feedback and organisational learning: what, following such writers as Kline and Rosenberg, we have referred to interactive 'chain-linked' models of innovation (Kline and Rosenberg, 1986; Lundvall and Tomlinson, 2002, p 216). Such integration may establish a virtuous dynamics by means of which an enterprise, a region or a country can accelerate along the path to a knowledge-based economy.

We have however succeeded at most in beginning to identify indicators of such processes. As we acknowledged in Chapter 4, these cumulative processes may need treatment in terms of system dynamics (Checkland and Scholes, 1990; Coyle, 1996; Powell and Bradford, 1998; 2000) and, perhaps, self-organising complex systems (Krugman, 1991; Byrne, 1998; Ball, 2004; Vidgen and Wang, 2004). This latter literature holds out the promise of formal modelling in terms of key variables which could in principle be captured in terms of statistical indicators. It also gives full recognition to the context – the 'control parameters' – within which these self-organising processes develop: just as throughout our discussion we have stressed the institutional contexts within which dynamic innovation unfolds and the consequent variety of trajectories of the knowledge-based economy.

Nevertheless, this promise is by no means assured. The literature on self-organising complex systems, in so far as it develops formal modelling, normally relies on simple models of agent interaction according to some fixed rules and can then trace the dynamics and emergent properties of the system at a macro-level. This is only with difficulty applied to our own interest in actors who scan the global horizon for threats, opportunities and good practice; who commit to lifelong learning so that their skills and capacities are regularly renewed; who contest politically the institutional framework within which this dynamic innovation proceeds and the distribution of its dividends.

Measurement

The new knowledge-based economy is not only difficult to model, it also poses specific difficulties for measurement. These measurement problems are of concern both for researchers, seeking to articulate empirical data with their conceptual models, and for those who are practically involved – enterprises, policy makers, etc – seeking to keep track of socio-economic transactions and transformations.

One area of difficulty relates to hedonics. As noted in Chapter 3, this refers to the difficulty of measuring – in this context – the quality of ICT inputs into the production process, in circumstances where that quality is rapidly advancing. As we saw in Chapter 6, analogous problems arise in relation to the measurement of human capital inputs, in circumstances where competencies and skills are rapidly being made obsolete. To take these discussions further is however beyond the scope of the present work.[1]

A second area of difficulty concerns the measurement of intangible assets. Such assets are not peculiar to a modern economy. However, knowledge-related intangible assets now form a very substantial and growing part of the resources held both by individual enterprises and by nations and it is around the control of such assets that competitive struggles increasingly focus (Eustace, 2004a). Difficulties and disagreements as to how to measure them are a growing impediment for business accountants, public policy makers, official statisticians and academic researchers. In fast-innovating new economy environments, these difficulties are compounded by the rapidity with which existing patents and innovations are 'creatively' destroyed by new ones, and the continuous dissolution and reforming of the teams in which much of this knowledge – tacit as well as formal – inheres.

Among the major intangible assets of corporations are those associated with intellectual property – patents, licenses etc – and which can be bought and sold, licensed and traded, just like physical goods (Hill, 2004). These are now being given explicit and standardised recognition through the International Financial Reporting Standards (IFRS) which have applied to listed EU companies since January 2005, after having been piloted in the US (Eustace, 2004a).

Education and knowledge are also intangible assets, held within households. However, existing systems of national accounts regard expenditures on education as a form of consumption rather than investment. As seen in Chapter 6, human capital is commonly measured in terms of the years of schooling or in terms of the skills and competencies acquired: there are however no established procedures for measuring it as an economic accounting asset. With the growth in the importance of such assets for the economy, the businesses within it and the individual, the accounting and statistical communities are urgently wrestling with what should be done (Hill, 2004). One obvious step forward national statisticians may be the development of 'satellite accounts' which would compute estimates of knowledge and human capital, without however at this stage challenging the assumptions underlying the systems of national accounts as such (De Haan, 2004).

Intangibles include not only the assets held within corporations and households, but also 'macro-intangibles': the contextual and institutional factors of the 'national innovation system' which can foster dynamic innovation. In Chapter 4, in reviewing the existing literatures, we took note of some of the elements of these systems, although in subsequent chapters it has been apparent that available indicators are overly crude. There is some evidence of the importance of business R&D investment and regulatory environment, for example, for dynamic innovation, but the analytical underpinnings are not robust (Eustace, 2004a).

Appraisal of indicator sets

In preceding chapters we have taken stock of a wide range of indicators of the new knowledge-based economy: some of them in routine use, others still being developed, under a variety of auspices. Notwithstanding the difficulties of modelling and measurement which we have just discussed, what overall appraisal can we now venture of the indicators sets that are currently in use for tracking the new knowledge-based economy? In particular, what judgement can we make on the EU indicator sets to which we have regularly referred in the course of the preceding chapters?

As we saw in Chapter 2, these EU indicator sets include three in particular. The *e*Europe 2005 indicators focus principally on the levels of connection to the internet by consumers and business and the degree to which e-commerce, e-government, e-health and e-education have developed (Table 2.1). The Science and Technology indicators of the European Research Area (ERA) refer to research capacity and activity levels, and the impact of this research activity within the national economy (Table 2.2). The European Innovation Scoreboard adds various indicators of innovation, including innovation activities by small and medium-sized enterprises (Table 2.3).

To appraise them – and to look beyond them – has been a principal task of this book. This appraisal has been principally in terms of their resonance with our conceptual modelling of the knowledge-based economy and their usefulness to policy makers. It has not made systematic reference to the other aspects of indicator and statistical quality with which statistical offices in particular have to be concerned, including their reliability, their comparability across countries and their timeliness. Nor has it considered the trade-offs which the producers and users of statistics may make among these different aspects of quality.[2] Nevertheless, it is clear that the pace of socio-economic change makes some of these trade-offs particularly pressing: for example, that between timeliness and accuracy.

Chapters 5-7 applied our conceptual model, with its four stages of innovation, across three domains. How well did these various EU indicators sets perform, in providing conceptually resonant indicators of readiness, intensity, impact and outcomes of the innovation process? The Science and Technology indicators and the European Innovation Scoreboard include many indicators referring to the skilled human resources and knowledge creation efforts which underpin innovation, even if they are defined in fairly broad terms. These were of particular interest for Stage 1 of our conceptual model; the human resource indicators are also of interest for Stage 4, as far as the outcomes of education and training are concerned. The *e*Europe indicators are helpful in tracking the penetration of the new technologies across economy and society: these are of interest to both Stage 1 and Stage 3. In regards to households they also illuminate patterns of use of online services, as we saw in Chapter 7.

Beyond that, however, these indicator sets are of only limited value. They have little to say about the organisational transformations involved in the knowledge-based economy, even though these are crucial in determining the ways in which the new technologies are used and the trajectories of socio-economic development which enterprises and communities traverse. The European Innovation Scoreboard includes indicators of innovation intensity which could be relevant to Stage 2: however, these focus on SMEs in particular, where the innovation capacity is generally rather weak, except when there are substantial supportive infrastructures. In regards to such infrastructures the EU indicators sets are however silent.

Our discussion in Chapters 5-7 went beyond these EU indicator sets and pointed to a variety of other sources, both governmental and private, from which additional indicators can be drawn. Nevertheless, it is evident that for each of these domains there remain major gaps: some of these will require substantial further conceptual and methodological work. As we have seen, one important such gap is indicators which could capture, at the micro-level, the intersections and interrelationships among the various elements of the new economy – ICT investment, human skills, organisational change and entrepreneurship – which make for dynamic change.

In reaching towards a set of indicators that span the process of innovation and are in some sense 'complete', we have also however to pose the question of parsimony. How far, in other words, is it possible to distil an array of indicators of this sort into a shorter list of 'headline' indicators which capture more economically but with little loss of information the phenomenon in question? This is a regular plea from policy makers, even if researchers attempting to conceptualise and measure the new economy are forced to acknowledge its complexity and call simultaneously for a wider range of more sophisticated indicators.

There are several well-established methodologies for achieving greater parsimony (Ramprakash, 2004). One is to analyse the variance among the indicators, in order to compress them into a smaller number of orthogonal indicators, which nevertheless capture most of the variance of the original set. This is an approach which depends upon the statistical analysis of empirical data sets, something which we are not here in a position to undertake.

A second approach is to create composite or synthetic indicators (OECD and Joint Research Council (JRC), 2004). This is, indeed, an approach used in both the European Innovation Scoreboard (EIS) and the Science and Technology indicators. The former involves seventeen indicators, selected to summarise the main drivers and outputs of innovations, divided into four groups; but also a composite innovation index, which provides a summary index of comparative progress, among the member states but also by reference to the USA and Japan (European Commission, 2002j). The latter involves four main themes and, for each theme, several key indicators – fifteen in all – against which the performance and progress of each member state are tracked. It also involves two composite indicators – investment in, and performance of, the knowledge-based economy – which are intended to provide 'headline' indicators of comparative progress (European Commission, 2002b). In both cases the construction of composite indicators may be defended as a summary measure and in terms of parsimony. Nevertheless, the methodological basis for these composite indicators is not entirely apparent. Certainly our own conceptual model hardly provides a clear theoretical justification for such an exercise (including for example the weights to be assigned to different components).

A third approach is to rely on expert judgements to choose a set of headline indicators, supported by a variety of supplementary indicators. This avoids suppressing the supplementary indicators; and it allows headline and supplementary indicators to be promoted and demoted, as policy interests change. It is this approach to parsimony that we would favour. It is consistent with the broader recognition that indicators can be appraised only in relation to the analytical or policy purposes that they serve, and, therefore, the policy actors in whom the governance of such policies is vested. It is to these purposes and governance that we turn in the next chapter.

Conclusion

As far as the selection of statistical indicators is concerned, our main focus in this book has been upon national and European statistical agencies and the policy directorates in government which are their immediate customers. However, with the new economy being driven forward at breakneck speed, primarily by private sector actors, public policy makers and their statistical services are barely able to keep up.

One response has been for policy makers to make use of 'quick and dirty' surveys, exemplified by some of the Eurobarometer surveys that have figured in some of the previous pages, providing a quick snapshot of developments in *e*Europe. As noted in the preceding section, this underlines the difficult trade-off between timeliness and accuracy posed by the pace of socio-economic change for the production of statistical information for public policy purposes.

Private sector actors gather data of their own, both about their internal operations and about the wider socio-economic environment in which they operate: and they do this as an integral part of their knowledge management systems. The indicators generated by these street level innovators merit attention alongside those to be found in official sources. Indeed, given the rapid processes of change within the new economy, and the difficulties faced by official statistical agencies in developing and delivering timely statistics based on conceptually resonant indicators, it is arguable that a fundamental reappraisal is needed of the relationship between private actors and public bodies, as far as the collection and provision of statistical information is concerned. To these issues we return in the final chapter of this book.

NINE

Benchmarking and governance

Introduction

In Chapter 2 we examined the Lisbon strategy for turning the European Union into "the most competitive and dynamic knowledge-based economy in the world, capable of sustaining economic growth with more and better jobs and greater social cohesion". At the centre of this strategy were procedures for policy benchmarking among the member states, intended to promote policy convergence and the exchange of best practice but without enlarging the areas of policy which were an EU competence.

We also recognised, however, that within this Lisbon strategy there was a basic ambiguity (see also Room, 2005). The process is in part the offspring of monetary union: as such it seeks to extend similar disciplines to a broader range of policy areas which are important for the attainment of a competitive knowledge-based economy. Growth and stability are therefore key objectives of Lisbon, just as they were of Maastricht. It was by reference to those policy concerns that in Chapter 3 we considered the challenges to conventional economic analysis of growth and stability that are posed by the new economy, and the difficulty in defining appropriate benchmarking indicators.

However, Lisbon also affirmed that in order to develop a knowledge-based economy, the member states of the EU would need to accelerate the transfer of technological and organisational know-how from the best performers to the rest of the Community. Benchmarking provides intelligence about different national experiences, it enriches national debates and it enables political and economic actors on the ground to drive the process of comparison and policy learning, depending on their specific needs and interests. Dynamic learning and innovation are the key objectives. It was by reference to these policy concerns that in Chapters 5 to 7 we sought appropriate benchmarking indicators in relation to enterprises, education and training, access and inclusion.

Of course, it can be cogently argued that these two sets of policy objectives – growth and stability, dynamic learning and innovation – are complements rather than being in conflict. Nevertheless, their emphases are different and so are their implications for the practice of benchmarking. It is likely to be only by appreciating their respective implications that they can be reconciled in practice.

What is in any event clear is that a simple and mechanical approach to benchmarking by reference to checklists of indicators is unlikely to assist in the move to a dynamic knowledge-based economy. As we have seen in preceding chapters, innovation requires the skilful bringing together of technological, human and organisational inventiveness and a 'learning organisation' that is continuously alert to the enhancement of its performance. If this is a requirement at the level of the enterprise or the public service, it is likely also to be a requirement at the level of the nation.

Benchmarking for dynamic change

Statistical indicators enable benchmarking, within a process of policy learning and the emulation of best practice. However, policy learning is not to be promoted through benchmarking alone. The Lisbon process is intended to bring together benchmarking, the identification and exchange of best practice, and peer review. The open method of coordination depends on a subtle and creative process involving these different elements.

This approach is evident in some of the EU initiatives related to the new knowledge-based economy. Thus, for example, in reference to the European Innovation Scoreboard, the European Commission foresees that as well as the indicators and benchmarks of the scoreboard, there will be a database of comparable information on national policy measures and workshops for sharing best practices in innovation policy: these three instruments are to provide the tools for 'intelligent' policy benchmarking. Benchmarking thus needs to be accompanied by 'benchlearning', involving the exchange of narratives, case studies and 'stories', which integrate these indicators into coherent accounts of how change practically occurs (European Commission, 2001g, Part III; 2002b, pp 5-6; 2003f, para 2.4). These narratives are in part intuitive; they embody a range of tacit knowledge; they recognise complexity and unpredictability; they tap into the specificities of national context and the path dependencies these involve, as well as the strategic choices being made by different actors (Lundvall and Tomlinson, 2002, pp 203, 207). This is, in turn, consistent with broader recent debates on innovation and policy learning, which offer a more adequate theory of policy learning than the mere comparison of national performances by reference to a series of indicators (Senge, 1990; Bennett, 1991; Dolowitz and March, 1996; Evans and Davies, 1999).

It is, moreover, important to recognise that what counts as the 'best' performance is not unproblematic: there may be a variety of possible trajectories of new economy development, embodying different trade-offs among its various outcomes and requiring different sorts of policy intervention. Naïve imitation of the supposed best performers may involve an abdication of political choice, as well as a failure to recognise the institutional specificities of the 'best' performer and the imitator. It may even be detrimental to high rates of innovation: diversity rather than imitation is likely to be productive of future innovation; and convergence of practices may create greater instability (Lundvall and Tomlinson, 2002). An approach to benchmarking and indicators which stresses alternative futures and political choice may therefore not only avoid the unthinking embrace of a single future, it may also promote the dynamism and innovation on which the new economy depends.

Benchmarking for political choice

Benchmarking raises questions about political choice. Are these comparisons of national performance, by reference to indicators and benchmarks, intended to track the progress of member states towards a single common future, and one which can be defined by reference to common economic and technological requirements? In this case the role of political leaders is limited to ensuring as rapid and comfortable an adjustment as possible to that future. Alternatively, are these comparisons intended to provide national policy makers with an array of different scenarios of potential development, to enrich national political debates about these alternative futures, and to provide guidance as to the policy interventions that might be made, in order to achieve one future rather than another? This suggests a quite different role for political leaders, making real political choices and trade-offs, on the basis of coordinated intelligence about different national experiences.

EU reports which benchmark the new knowledge-based economy give little sense of alternative patterns of socio-economic development and trade-offs. The language used is that of laggards catching up with leaders, with the implication that those leaders hold out the future to which the laggards must adjust. Nevertheless, there would seem to be no reason why, in principle, the selected benchmarking indicators should not be used to reveal the trade-offs among alternative outcomes and, therefore, a variety of possible futures. Do higher rates of competitiveness through technological innovation have to be traded against higher risks of social inclusion? Do high rates of social inclusion in the new economy presuppose high rates of investment in human capital? This type of exercise is consistent with studies such as that by Ferrera et al (2000), undertaken in the lead-up to Lisbon, analysing the policy trade-offs of precisely this sort that have been made by different EU member states. It is also, of course, common in comparative policy studies, where outcome indicators are examined by reference to a variety of antecedent factors (see, for example, Wilensky, 1975). At present, however, this seems to be somewhat peripheral to the Lisbon process.

However, as for example Lundvall and Tomlinson argue, notwithstanding the success of the US in relation to the new economy, it would be wrong to assume that the EU has no alternative but to copy that experience. On the contrary, some of the smaller national economies within the EU demonstrate the scope for a very different type of 'new economy', involving positive policies of social inclusion, which draws "its strength from giving citizens security in [times of] change, ... building social capital [and] sharing the costs of change" (Lundvall and Tomlinson, 2002, p 227). More generally, as seen above, too much copying of the best performers may be problematic, not least for the move to a knowledge-based economy characterised by high rates of innovation.

Nevertheless, it is no easy matter to map these alternative trajectories of socio-economic development and the alternative futures that the new economy may offer. One approach might involve the elucidation of a variety of alternative scenarios of future socio-economic development of the knowledge society (see for example FISTERA, 2004) and their confrontation with our own analysis of the dynamics of innovation and transformation in the new economy. That is however beyond the scope of the present book.

Intelligent benchmarking for open governance

When the Lisbon process was launched in 2000, it envisaged a 10-year programme of dynamic reform. With the half-way point approaching, the EU at the end of 2004 began a review of the process with the Kok Report (European Commission, 2004a). As we noted in Chapter 2, the Kok report endorses and reaffirms the broad thrust of the Lisbon strategy, including the Open Method of Coordination, but concludes that by and large the strategy has had only limited success.

One of the main reasons, according to Kok, is that the Lisbon strategy has addressed too many policy areas, thereby lacking coherence and a clear sense of priorities. Much of the subsequent debate has therefore focused on bringing the different OMC processes together, streamlining them into a single process of national reporting (European Commission, 2005b). In regards more specifically to benchmarking, the report calls for a smaller number of simple indicators, more tightly applied, and with greater political costs – in terms of 'naming and shaming' – imposed on poorly performing countries. The imposition of these political costs is intended to strengthen the role of benchmarking as far as policy convergence and performance improvement are concerned; it is also intended to increase the accountability of governments to the collectively agreed EU process.

In light of the foregoing discussion, it is not at all clear that the Kok recommendations are well judged. A few simple indicators, imposed top-down as a set of goals to which all are committed, may be appropriate in the monetary field, or for the removal of the remaining barriers to the single market (European Commission, 2004a, p 24). They are less applicable elsewhere, if policy learning is the goal. Intelligent benchmarking is more likely to require bottom-up benchmarking, political choice by local and national actors among alternative socio-economic trajectories, and the selection by those actors of rather more sophisticated indicators of dynamic transformation.

This also involves a rather different notion of good governance from that of the Kok Report. As we saw in Chapter 2, the Lisbon process involved the EU moving into policy areas which had until then been rather jealously protected as a national preserve. These were also areas where policy goals were contested. The open method of coordination therefore recognised the role of a wide range of actors, not just national governments. This seems to have been driven in part by fears about the democratic deficit of EU policy making (European Commission, 2001b; Lebessis and Paterson, 2001). The ambiguities within the Lisbon process, and the role of benchmarks and indicators in illuminating alternative trajectories of socio-economic development, take on a particular significance, when viewed by reference to this debate on EU governance.

One common approach to these questions of EU governance is to examine how far the Open Method of Coordination is meeting the Lisbon expectation, that a wide variety of actors would be involved in shaping the processes of policy benchmarking – and, in the context of the present book, the specific indicators that are chosen. A variety of working parties and expert groups have indeed been consulted in the indicator-building processes of interest for this book (even if this has not differed greatly from traditional EU 'comitology'). Nevertheless, what is also needed is to examine how far the chosen indicators provide coordinated and transparent intelligence about different national experiences, on the basis of which policy makers can choose among alternative futures and trajectories of development, under full public scrutiny. In face of such scrutiny, domestic political leaders could no longer rely on the relative ignorance of their population regarding practices elsewhere: they would, instead, need to justify their performance by comparison with best practice in other countries.

Social benchmarking of this sort could have crucial consequences for their political credibility. It would also constitute a powerful commitment to good governance on the part of the EU: for while it would affirm national responsibility, it would also affirm Community interest in how that national responsibility is exercised (see also De la Porte et al, 2001, pp 300-1). This is a far cry from the sort of good governance – naming and shaming – enjoined by the Kok Report. How far other developments in the knowledge-based economy promote this active scrutiny of public policy making by the public is of course a separate question. As we saw in Chapter 7, there has been widespread concern at the apparently declining levels of civic engagement across advanced western societies. Nevertheless, as we also saw, there is some evidence that e-democracy represents a positive force for re-engagement.

To conclude this section, it is worth taking note of the implications of this discussion – and indeed of the preceding chapters – for current debates about European citizenship. The Lisbon process was set in motion at a time when there was much debate about the significance and meaning of such European citizenship. This was in part a debate about the rights and entitlements that the individual citizen enjoyed in relation to European – rather than national – institutions. It was also a debate about the 'democratic deficit' of the EU (Lebessis and Paterson, 2001).

The Lisbon process aimed in part to continue the process of European economic integration: widening economic opportunities, stimulating job creation and removing national barriers to Europe-wide enterprise. As far as individuals were concerned, this meant an enrichment of economic or civil rights (Marshall, 1950). Meanwhile, the removal of discrimination in the enjoyment of these rights continued: not only in relation to gender but also, under the Amsterdam Treaty, in relation to a wide range of other lines of inequality.

The Lisbon process was also, however, concerned to guarantee a measure of social security at a time of economic turbulence, if only to maintain social peace. The social dimension of Lisbon extended also to human investment, seen as a key resource for the knowledge-based economy, but also a crucial guarantee of social inclusion. The findings emerging from Chapters 6 and 7 are consistent with this approach. Strong social rights, providing a measure of economic security and ensuring wide participation in education and training, are crucial to economic progress and social cohesion. This emphasis is not however apparent in the Kok report or in some of the Commission documents that have been published in its aftermath (European Commission, 2005e). Security against terror is rightly stressed as the context for the exercise of political freedom; but social security as the context for economic freedom does not receive the same priority.

Finally, as we have seen, the Lisbon process has posed questions about the accountability and governance: in other words, about the political rights of citizenship. The Kok report appears to see improved governance as involving tighter upward accountability of member states in relation to the benchmarking processes of Lisbon. Against this, we have asked whether benchmarking could, rather, support public scrutiny of national policies by reference to best practice in other countries.

In whatever ways the Lisbon process is re-engineered for the second half of the decade, these questions about European citizenship will remain as a point of reference for debates about European policy development.

Conclusion

If benchmarking of the new knowledge-based economy and policy learning are to be 'intelligent', they must deploy a range of tools proportionate to its complexity. They must also illuminate the alternative patterns of socio-economic development that may be available and the trade-offs involved. The extent to which these *desiderata* are met has major implications for governance in the EU. Such are the findings that emerge from the foregoing discussion.

Benchmarking, policy learning, political choice and the pursuit of particular trajectories of socio-economic development all presuppose a certain level of State capacity. Capacity-building is, indeed, an integral part of the Lisbon strategy, as countries are encouraged to build on best practice and Community programmes are refashioned to support achievement of the Lisbon goals. This does not however mean that the necessary improvements to State capacity can be painlessly absorbed. As Petmesidou and Mossialos (2005) have argued, Greece in particular appears to be institutionally deadlocked: frozen in pre-modern forms of social and political integration that deform social rights, undermine state capacity and block any domestic reform process in response to European initiatives. This is perhaps an extreme case: but the warnings from the Kok report suggest that institutional deadlocks are by no means a Greek monopoly.

Benchmarking is meant to inform policy intervention in the new knowledge-based economy, with a view to accelerating trajectories of transformation. This policy environment is however multitiered, with the principal actors distributed variously at sub-national, national, European and international levels (Kaiser and Prange, 2004). Benchmarking at national level alone — as is predominantly the case within the Open Method of Coordination — may acknowledge the formal responsibility of national governments for the policy domains which have been left outside the Community mandate, but this does not necessarily accord with the multitiered environment in which policy is actually implemented. Nor does it acknowledge the multitiered context — regional, national, European and international — within which the new economy is developing (Soete, 1999 section 4).

We acknowledged the importance of the regional (i.e. sub-national) level in our discussion of enterprises in Chapter 5 (see also Wolfe, 2000). Local and regional networks and clusters are being reconfigured in face of the new technologies of communication but they are still of significance for economic dynamism, as therefore also are policies concerned with regional capacity building. In our final chapter we go on to consider the linkages among the national, European and global levels, and the implications for policy benchmarking.

TEN

Globalisation and the knowledge economy

Introduction

As we saw in Chapter 1, when setting the context for this study, the development of the new knowledge-based economy is intimately bound up with the process of globalisation (see, for example, Soete, 1999; Togati, 2002). The ICT revolution enables enormously greater speed and accuracy of communication, transcending national boundaries and permitting greatly increased transparency of markets worldwide. These global markets then foster more intense competition, driving technological and organisational innovation and reshaping the global division of labour and welfare. They pose new challenges for the regulation of commerce and the protection of intellectual property rights.

Any attempt to conceptualise and measure the new economy must acknowledge this transformation of the international political economy. This does not mean that processes of globalisation are an outworking of the new economy alone. The challenge is to understand the specific ways in which the new economy and processes of globalisation are interrelated.

Globalisation can be defined as the organisation of economic, social or other activity in terms which transcend – and may even ignore – national boundaries (Dasgupta, 1998; Held et al, 1999; Torres, 2001). It raises questions of governance: how shall this activity be subjected to political scrutiny and direction if the nation state – traditionally the principal mode of governance – can no longer exercise control of this activity by reference to its own boundaries? It also raises questions of information: how can public policy makers provide themselves with the statistical information they require for evidence-based policy, when the instruments which they have inherited for this purpose are still organised principally by reference to national boundaries?

Globalisation is only one element in the reorganisation of space that has been under way in recent decades. For the countries of the

EU, the effects of globalisation have to be set alongside those of Europeanisation, including monetary union and the Lisbon process, and the growing importance of the regions, at least in terms of governance. Nevertheless, the principal focus in this final chapter will be upon globalisation and the new economy, with these additional dimensions of spatial reorganisation being addressed only in so far as they are relevant to that discussion.

Benchmarking for national action

Once again, our starting point is the Lisbon process. Lisbon places national governments at the centre of attention. (The same, indeed, goes for the reports produced by most other international organisations, including the OECD and the UN.) Benchmarks and indicators are defined in terms which allow national comparisons and each government is affirmed as responsible for its own progress and choices.

The previous chapter considered the extent of those choices. It asked whether the indicators employed in the Lisbon process were intended to provide benchmarks of progress towards the new economy, seen as a single, technologically-determined future, or to help policy makers and their publics in choosing among alternative new economy futures. It suggested that the aim should be to equip national policy makers with indicators that enable them to benchmark their neighbours, but with the aim of choosing their own particular socio-economic trajectory.

This argument can now be turned on its head. The Lisbon process places national governments at the centre of attention: benchmarks and indicators are defined in terms which allow them to be used for monitoring and comparing the progress of individual countries. This is also consistent with the traditional remit of Eurostat, to support and complement the national statistical institutes and the data they produce. The problem is that this distracts attention from the global processes that, to an increasing extent, are shaping the dynamics of socio-economic development. The less light that is shed on those processes, the less scope there is for political action – whether at national or supranational level – to reshape them. The more likely it then is, that individual countries will indeed have little choice but to adjust to a future that appears to them to be a technological necessity.

Much of this global socio-economic transformation is driven less by technology than by the multinational enterprises (MNEs) who dominate that technology. They undertake the lion's share of industrial innovation and dominate the intangible knowledge-based assets of the new economy. Much of this activity is, however, internal to these corporations: it therefore does not appear in the national accounts of the countries across whose borders their operations range, or in the statistics of internationally traded services. Individual national statistical offices catch only a glimpse of this global activity, as it passes through their strictly national data tools. This is important because without such indicators, it becomes difficult to track the extent to which innovation is concentrated within a few rich countries: it also denies national policy makers the information base they require, when considering the scope for building up their national innovation systems in partnership with locally-based MNEs.

The new information technologies also enable MNEs – and advanced industrial countries – more easily to out-source low value added activities to developing countries. Some activities (such as call centres) do not need to be located physically close to the main agglomerations of science and technological innovation and there may be a substantial labour cost advantage in out-sourcing. In addition, there may be advantages in out-sourcing activities which are pollution-generating, but which are tolerated by the lighter regulatory regimes of developing countries. Thus while MNEs may be well-placed to range freely across national boundaries, this does not mean that such boundaries are irrelevant to them: on the contrary, their global strategies can be carefully chosen, having regard to the different sets of opportunities that are afforded by the conditions in each country. These strategies are however by no means transparent to the countries concerned. The overall effect is that the 'knowledge-based economy' could become increasingly opaque, with many of the communities affected facing growing risks of exclusion from political and cultural participation in decisions to shape its direction.

In considering the sorts of indicators that the Lisbon process should utilise, we are therefore inevitably led also to consider questions of governance: the governance of global activity, but also of the statistical information about this global activity that policy makers will require, if they are to expose the socio-economic futures that their societies confront, and if they are to identify the scope for intervention to shape those futures. If the indicators that are made available persist in treating the nation state as being in charge of its own destiny, the result will be nation states which are less well equipped to act in concert, to shape their shared socio-economic environment. To this extent, even such control of their fates as they can still expect to exercise will be needlessly undermined.

Statistical indicators for a global order

What system of indicators would give visibility to the global value chains of the knowledge-based economy, the associated movements of factors of production, and the changing patterns of domination and exclusion to which communities around the world are exposed?

Globalisation, we have argued, is the organisation of economic, social or other activity in terms which transcend national boundaries. Those social, economic and political actors whose strategies span this global terrain can shape the ways in which the new economy develops and the distribution of its dividends. This global activity has different consequences for different communities, including national communities. It not only shapes the international division of labour and welfare, it also sends these communities along different trajectories of socio-economic development, fateful for their future capacities and security. It is for this reason that robust statistics of these dividends and trajectories are required, for without them national policy makers cannot lay bare the political options that face their societies.

As seen above, MNEs are of particular significance, for three interrelated reasons. First, because they are par excellence global players, developing strategies which span the global terrain, as they build global value chains. They also have access to larger knowledge stocks, with important implications for their capacity to innovate (Criscuola et al, 2004). Second, because much of the technological and organisational innovation associated with the new economy – and the transfers of knowledge assets between countries – goes on within them (Clayton, 2004a). Third, because much of this activity, being 'internal' to a given MNE, does not show up in conventional national statistics: not because statistical definitions and categories are simply outdated, but because of the intrinsic problems associated with national authorities obtaining data internal to a multinational operation (Eustace, 2004a).

Indicators of cross-border movements

The new economy is accelerating the mobility of capital, skilled labour and services across frontiers. National and international statistics are only slowly adjusting to handle these mobile factors. National governments and international organisations are however now making moves to establish more appropriate definitions and data standards. Whether this will go far enough, in terms of capturing changing patterns of economic, social and technological domination, remains to be seen.

The OECD is spearheading this drive: recent publications grapple with the methodological problems involved and provide such data as are currently available. Thus, for example, *OECD Science, Technology and Industry Outlook*, deals *inter alia* with the globalisation of science and technology and with cross-border human capital flows (OECD, 2004g). *Counting Immigrants and Expatriates in OECD Countries* is concerned with migration flows between industrialised countries (OECD, 2004b), while *Migration of Highly Skilled Indians* OECD (2004d) tracks the global movement of brainpower, including IT workers and health professionals, from a major developing country to the advanced world. The OECD (2005) *Handbook on Economic Globalisation Indicators* is concerned with MNEs in relation to trade, international investment and technology transfer. It proposes indicators that will better disentangle and treat consistently the cross-national transactions between parent companies and affiliates, the flows of investment and the patterns of ultimate beneficial ownership. It does the same in relation to the internationalisation of industrial R&D, the international diffusion of technology and trade in high technology products.

National policy makers cannot afford to ignore the consequences of these flows for national economic strength and prospects. There is a specific driver in taxation: national statistical systems are expected to enable governments to monitor and measure economic activity, and to adjust the fiscal system to cope with new sources of wealth. There is also a political need to respond to the fears of electorates that these cross-border flows may pose a threat to their future economic security. Under political pressure from this domestic constituency, fearful of jobs haemorrhaging as MNEs relocate their operations offshore, the US Bureau of Economic Analysis has argued for direct surveys of multinational corporations and their global activities (US Bureau of Economic Analysis, 2003, para 41). New data instruments throw light on many aspects of MNE behaviour, including their contribution to cross-border transfer of technology and the extent, for example, to which their location decisions are geared to lighter regimes of environmental regulation (paras 18-19, 30). This leaves some issues still unresolved, including the statistical treatment of the intellectual capital residing within individual MNEs, but treated as the shared asset of the corporation in question, without regard to national boundaries (UK ONS, 2003, Section III: see also the discussion in Chapter 8 above). Nevertheless, it at least raises the possibility that the reporting requirements placed on MNEs might become much more substantial than at present (where annual reports to the regulatory authority of the country in which the MNE is registered are all that is strictly required).

Indicators of global development

Indicators of global development are commonplace. At first glance therefore it might seem unhelpful to suggest that the lack of such indicators is a significant element of the opacity of the 'knowledge-based economy'. Thus, for example, the World Bank publishes annually a *World Development Report*, which includes data relating to the knowledge economy and recognises its central place in global development: see in particular World Bank (1999). Similarly, the UN produces an annual *Human Development Report*: the 2001 report was concerned in particular with "making new technologies work for human development" (United Nations, 2001).

With more specific reference to ICT, the UN Millennium Development Goals take as one of their targets "in cooperation with the private sector to make available the benefits of new technologies, specifically information and communications". Corresponding indicators are being used to track the progress of the different UN member states (ITU, 2003, ch 4). The World Summit on the Information Society, and its co-sponsor the International Telecommunications Union (ITU), already introduced in Chapter 1, have also been active in producing indicators and statistics of the global digital divide and the prospects for extending to the developing world some of the benefits of the new knowledge economy. The ITU's digital access index goes beyond technology infrastructure to include affordability and education and takes account of four fundamental factors that shape a country's ability to access ICTs: infrastructure, affordability, knowledge and quality (Minges, 2003). Meanwhile the World Economic Forum has been producing a series of *Global Information Technology Reports,* which among other things monitor and compare the 'networked readiness' of different countries, by reference to indicators of internet use on the one hand, ICT infrastructure and environment on the other (World Economic Forum, 2004).

Nevertheless, what all these initiatives do is to report the progress of individual nations – or groups of nations – in respect of a list of common indicators of social, technological and economic progress. This is valuable, indeed indispensable for public debate and policy making in the international arena. However, these indicators do not adequately capture the global processes and transformations which to a considerable degree shape the fates of these nations and the place that they are able to occupy within the international division of labour and welfare. What is also needed are indicators showing how the new economy shapes the international division of labour and welfare, and sends communities along different trajectories of socio-economic development, fateful for their future capacities and security.

These might for example refer to the networks and agglomerations around which this global economy develops. The new economy exerts its potential in part by enabling the building of networks of unrivalled scope and with unrivalled speed. The growth of a network provides its members with increasing returns, and makes it increasingly costly not to join, albeit membership comes at the price of hegemonic lock-in. Indicators are needed of the global dominance of particular networks within the new economy. Thus, for example, databases are available, updated throughout the year, concerned with the world's largest internet backbones, the traffic they carry and the providers who operate them (Meijers, 2003; PriMetrica, 2003). These also serve to identify those cities that are the hubs, and those that are the spokes which interconnect the major economic blocks. These could be taken as indicators of the relative power positions of different cities and regions within the global new economy.

One element of such networks is the setting of standards. Challenges to the international supremacy of particular new economy standards are therefore of potential interest, especially if they can be expressed as indicators of the degree of universal domination that such standards enjoy. In this context, it is interesting to notice the growing insistence of China on its own software standards (*New York Times,* 13 January 2004) and the reluctance of India to accede to OECD standards in respect of IPR (where standard setting is of the greatest importance for the expansion of internet-based applications).

The new economy requires for its development agglomerations of appropriate managerial expertise, a highly skilled workforce, the exchange of tacit know-how, social capital and trust, well-connected into the national and international innovation system and the communication technologies of the new economy. The global dynamics of the new economy determine where these agglomerations are located and which communities will reap the benefits.[1] Different stages of our innovation model, as set out in Chapter 4, may have different relationships to these knowledge agglomerations and may therefore be located in different countries, through foreign affiliates and the operations of MNEs.

Indicators of these emerging agglomerations are needed. This is not at all the same as indicators showing the extent to which different countries and regions have gained access to, or are making use of, particular elements of the new economy, as these progressively diffuse. It is, instead, identifying those regions and countries which, by virtue of their existing agglomerations of knowledge resources, are at the leading edge of new waves of innovation, reinforcing their competitive advantage.

Indicators of dependency upon these agglomerations are also important: with particular communities finding that their own preferred patterns of socio-economic development are distorted by those of more powerful agglomerations, and that the very attempt to become connected into the new economy only serves, initially at least, to disempower them. There is a growing literature on these forms of 'adverse incorporation' into the global new economy that are experienced by developing countries (see, for example, Humphrey et al, 2003). Similar effects may also become apparent among the EU accession countries, where levels of infrastructural development are significantly different from those of existing members (as previously discussed in Chapter 7, Stage 1). It is not at all self-evident that benchmark indicators measuring national performance against common standards will readily pick up these unequal relationships and their distortion of the socio-economic futures facing peripheral economies.

Opportunities for change

There is no authoritative supranational public body with the mandate to collect statistical information about these global transformations. Eurostat, the OECD and the UN set standards for statistical work and bring together data from different member states, but beyond this they hardly provide a statistical monitoring of the global environment as such.

Efforts to build a more adequate statistical order at the global level will clearly depend crucially upon the stance taken by MNEs. We have referred to the efforts by some governments – notably that of the US – to develop direct surveys of MNEs and their global activities. It remains an open question as to whether national political authorities, even acting in concert, will have the authority to secure such reporting by MNEs in reliable and consistent terms. Nevertheless, MNEs and their operations are of course by no means disconnected from national governments: on the contrary, it is the alliances between MNEs and the governments of the wealthiest industrial nations that give them their power (see for example Dahlberg, 2002).

Moreover, MNEs, concerned to maintain their public reputations – another of the 'intangible assets' which may be difficult to measure but are nevertheless weighty – are by no means immune to pressure from their customers and shareholders. Corporate social responsibility, involving respect for social and environmental standards, enforced down the whole value chain that an MNE manages, is more than mere rhetoric, even if external enforcement of this responsibility – by civil society and the EU for example – is only 'soft' (European Commission, 2002d). Such corporate social responsibility has in recent years been the basis of the UN Secretary-General's Global Compact: a voluntary accord into which MNEs are invited to enter, but one which many corporations appear to view as a prized attestation of their probity (www.unglobalcompact. org: see also the Global Reporting Initiative www.globalreporting. org). Such a compact already involves a commitment to regular reporting and transparency: on such a commitment it might be possible to construct a more elaborate and systematic statistical order at global level.

Meanwhile, in the world of financial accounting post-Enron, a similar joint commitment has emerged, on the part of governments, financial regulators and corporations, to secure public confidence through more robust and transparent accounting procedures. This is by no means driven from the side of government alone. Nor indeed is it driven solely by US interests, notwithstanding their dominant position within the world economy. The lead has been taken by the International Accounting Standards Board (IASB), a private body, but this has succeeded in capturing the support of a broad-based coalition of governmental and business organisations, thereby straddling the interests of business and public policy (Porter, 2004). This is no surprise. Quite apart from pressures coming from national governments, consumers and shareholders, and civil society, MNEs have a strong interest in securing an orderly and transparent international trading environment.

In short, therefore, it is at least an open question whether a new compact could be built, on a global basis, between governments, intergovernmental organisations, MNEs and civil society, to develop a more transparent and timely system of public information and indicators which capture the dynamics of global socio-economic transformation, along the lines suggested in the previous section of this chapter. Social pacts of this sort are by no means easy to construct (Fajertag and Pochet, 2000). Nevertheless, the progressive degradation of international public statistics that is otherwise in danger of occurring will impose costs on all the aforementioned actors: this provides a powerful incentive for joint action.

The global challenge

The Lisbon strategy was intended to build a Europe that could compete effectively with the US and Japan. However, if the Lisbon strategy remains focused on the internal dynamics of the EU economy, what it can achieve must remain severely limited. Global competition needs an appropriate institutional context, including an appropriate global regime of public statistics and indicators. To create this requires an essentially cooperative endeavour with these global rivals. The challenge therefore for the EU is to play a full part in constructing an international order which is transparent, rule-governed and accountable. This is inseparable from the quest for a dynamic knowledge-based economy at regional, national and European levels.

A global regime of public statistics and indicators, capable of capturing the dynamics of global transformation, can build on existing European and international experience of statistical collaboration. It must also however tap into the emerging patterns of corporate social responsibility and build a global statistical compact, in which business needs for a transparent international environment are met alongside public policy requirements. Such a regime could serve as an invaluable resource for comparing different national experiences of the knowledge-based economy and illuminating alternative trajectories of socio-economic development. It could thereby contribute to well-informed public debate, downward accountability and good governance. National, regional and international public institutions could win credit thereby (De la Porte et al, 2001).

The quest for a transparent, rule-governed and accountable international order can hardly be limited to the statistical domain. It has also to address processes of global socio-economic transformation which transcend the management capacity of even the most powerful nations: new systems of governance must be constructed, involving supranational authorities, nation states and the wider array of stakeholders in pluralist societies. This does not however mean that nation states are obsolete: on the contrary, such a regime could empower them. An important point of reference for such a global political settlement could be the Lisbon strategy itself, notwithstanding its ambiguities and limitations (Room, 2004). This would however challenge the neo-liberal orthodoxy of much international policy making on globalisation, tempering the flexibility and insecurity of the market with a strong agenda of social rights and an active public policy.

The benchmarks of the OMC, setting standards for action by national governments, already have their counterpart in such international standards as the ILO core labour standards and the Millennium Development Goals of the UN, albeit with less rigorous and systematic reporting. The OMC also includes mechanisms for cross-national policy learning and the exchange of good practice, in support of this standard-setting. Here again there are global counterparts, for example the technical assistance and capacity building offered by the ILO to enable developing countries to meet the core labour standards. The danger is that this transfer of policy lessons may be very one-sided, with the inappropriate imposition of western models on developing countries (Bevan, 2004). Finally, the coordination of national policy making in the EU involves support to countries in raising their policy performance, by means of resource transfers for investment, capacity building and skill development. Such transfers exist in the international realm and they are, of course, the ostensible *raison d'être* of international aid. There is, however, one crucial difference. In the EU, funds are allocated for such cross-national transfers on the basis of Community-wide taxation; the criteria on which they are to be distributed are decided by the Member States together; and to receive such funds, if the criteria are satisfied, is an entitlement rather than charity. Resource transfers to the developing world, far from being rule-based, can perhaps best be described as fragmented charity, in many cases being driven by the domestic agendas of donors from the rich world.

The question therefore is whether the EU experience of rule-based policy coordination, capacity-building and shared governance could and should find more solid reflection in the international arena. To rise to this challenge is likely to require major acts of political leadership by the EU institutions. Nevertheless, the global prospects for the European economy depend so heavily on establishing new patterns of equitable interdependence with trading partners worldwide, that the European policy debate can hardly avoid addressing the external consequences of its internal socio-economic strategy. This appears to be well understood, to judge by the efforts of the Commission to build coherence between these internal and external dimensions of European policy (European Commission DG Employment, 2001; 2005).

So much for the struggle over the institutional setting of socio-economic globalisation. This also then suggests a response to the debate with which this book began, concerned on the one hand with the extent to which contemporary processes of neo-liberal globalisation are bringing about a new phase of convergent development (Giddens, 1990; Castells, 2001), on the other with the mediation of these effects by national differences in socio-economic institutions, with a corresponding variety of development trajectories (Goldthorpe, 2001; Hall and Soskice, 2001). Previous chapters have emphasised the significance of different institutional contexts for the process of innovation; they have contested any assumption within the Lisbon process of a single common future, defined by common economic and technological requirements; they have instead argued for a variety of socio-economic futures and trajectories of development, involving real political choices. To this extent, our conclusions are closer to the 'varieties of capitalism' tradition of scholarship.

It is however not enough to acknowledge that the effects of globalisation are mediated through the prism of nationally distinctive socio-economic institutions and socio-political settlements. As seen above, it is also important to recognise that the institutional setting within which processes of global socio-economic transformation are embedded – the global socio-political settlement – is itself contested. What is more, many key actors are playing a variety of 'two-level games' across these local/national and global terrains, building power positions and seizing opportunities on one level, the better to pursue interests on the other (Kristensen and Zeitlin, 2005). For these actors, to construct a global order in their own image is a prize eminently worth pursuing. To cloak this order in the language of neo-liberalism, the 'European Social Model' or some other ideology may facilitate and legitimate the quest: but the process of globalisation and the forms of global governance remain essentially contested.

Endnotes

Chapter Three

1   This section is based on Winnett (2004a), which offers a lengthier and more technical treatment of these issues.

2   This section is based on Winnett (2004b), which offers a lengthier and more technical treatment of these issues.

Chapter Four

1   The significance of market size for the availability of external increasing returns is something emphasised by Kaldor in particular, following the earlier work of Allyn Young (Kaldor, 1985, ch 3). From this point of view, it is the rapid enlargement of markets that the new economy permits that is particularly important as a driver of increasing returns, technological innovation and productivity growth.

2   It follows that the significance of networks lies partly in their mobilisation of 'intangibles': these include the standards that networks embody, and that favour the next wave of inventions that network members release onto the market; they also include the knowledge base from which network members develop these new inventions, and whose prospective economic value the network enhances. To capture these intangibles in quantitative – or even monetary – indicators is fraught with difficulties (Eustace, 2004a); see also Chapter 8.

3   There may be indicators, such as those on multinational investment, outsourcing or trade content, which help to capture this. Nevertheless, especially at the initial stages of the innovation process, the national location of the entailed knowledge may be problematic: much is held by corporations operating transnationally, and the national accounting systems on which most indicators ultimately depend are ill-suited to deal with such transnational intangibles. See also Chapter 8 below.

4   See also the discussion by Clayton of the relationship between these stages of the innovation process, the building of global value chains by MNEs and the consequent – but in general unmeasured – transfers of knowledge between countries (Clayton, 2004a). In regards to the measurement of such transfers, see also Criscuolo

et al (2004), cited by Clayton, which assembles evidence that globally engaged enterprises are more able to tap into such transfers.

Chapter Five

1   The original INNFORM survey instrument is available at http://www.sagepub.co.uk/pdf/books/009754Appendix.pdf.
2   As background to the European Innovation Scoreboard, the Commission has produced an analysis of national innovation systems which attempts to analyse some of these institutional and contextual factors: European Commission (2003a). Nevertheless, the conclusions that emerge from this report are not robust.

Chapter Six

1   http://europa.eu.int/comm/enterprise/ict/policy/ict-skills.htm
2   Demand for skilled workers from other countries will be reduced to the extent that companies 'offshore' their operations to those countries (European Commission, 2004g, p 27). Data on offshoring are rather limited but are urgently required (US Department of Commerce, 2003, pp 30-31). An alternative or complementary strategy is to exploit the increased opportunities for offshore teleworking afforded by new telecommunication technologies, employing skilled workers from other countries but without requiring their physical movement to the European area (di Martino, 2001, Part III).
3   Alongside this need to track international movements of knowledge workers, there is also benefit in tracking such movements at the regional level (Bocconi, 2004). This may be particularly important in identifying bottlenecks which impede the development of agglomerations of knowledge-based industries.
4   For a discussion of some of the methodological and measurement problems involved, with particular reference to the use of labour force surveys, see OECD (2002b). It is worth adding that the level of skill which a particular job requires is not necessarily the same as the level of skill which those discharging such jobs have attained (Rose, 1994; 2003).
5   This is more than a matter just of pedagogical style. It must be understood by reference to a longer-standing critical literature concerned with the exercise and contestation of power within systems of education and training, and the place of education within the larger distribution of socio-economic power: see (Young, 1971; Bowles and Gintis, 1976; Bernstein, 1977; Bourdieu, 1977).

6   This is a key thesis underlying the European Commission's Communication: *The New Generation of Community Education and Training Programmes after 2006* (European Commission, 2004a) and the proposals it offers for new EU initiatives in the fields of education and training.

7   The growth of private universities is particularly evident in transitional and developing countries, where existing higher education infrastructures have been quite unable to cope with rapidly expanding demand (OBHE, 2004f).

8   It should not be supposed that this is a development confined to the advanced industrial nations. India, which has the ambition to become a 'knowledge super-power' by 2020, is reforming the legislative and administrative framework within which her universities work, in order to push them in an entrepreneurial, market-oriented direction, with greater attention to international student markets (OBHE, 2003a). Russia meanwhile has launched a Distance Learning Satellite Network offering courses world-wide: see (OBHE, 2004h).

9   Germany is a country where universities have long operated as public non-competitive institutions. Now, however, there are signs of change. Private state-approved higher education institutions are developing; Government is considering the creation of a small number of elite institutions; and there are pressures on universities to become more entrepreneurial and to enter the global market (OBHE, 2004c). So also, Denmark has introduced tuition fees for non-EU students, the first Scandinavian country to do so, and is moving to compete more actively in the market for international students (OBHE, 2004e).

10 See also the Bologna process web-site: http://www.bologna-bergen2005.no/

11 http://www.eua.be/eua/en/projects_quality.jspx

12 In the OECD database, cross-border e-learning and employee training provided by a foreign country are both included within a more general category: 'Miscellaneous business, professional and technical services' and cannot be separately identified. International trade statistics do not enable identification of earnings from the establishment of campuses and teaching facilities abroad. See Larsen et al (2001), paras 14-15.

13 Here is not perhaps the place to explore these issues at greater length. It is however worth adding that, even if Western exporters are limited to niche markets, these niche markets may have a disproportionate significance. In particular, it is evident that in

some countries at least, education in the medium of English, and if possible in Western institutions, is a key element in the efforts by elite groups to perpetuate their privileged position (Room, 2000): the restriction of Western institutions to niche markets is to be understood therefore in part by reference to the concern of such groups to monopolise and restrict access to domestic privilege and power.

Chapter Eight

1   For a more extended treatment, see Winnett (2004a).
2   For more extended discussion of these issues see Winnett, Room and Gould (2003).

Chapter Ten

1   There is a substantial literature concerned with the international location dynamics of high-skill, technologically-based economies (see, for example, Porter, 1990; Dunning, 1993b; Dunning, 1993a; Held et al, 1999). What this highlights is that far from capital seeking low cost countries in a 'race to the bottom', it tends to be attracted by agglomerations of knowledge resources and by national policies which strengthen them (Room, 2002). The development of the new economy can be set in this context of analysis, but with the pace of innovation dramatically accelerated and the implications for the trajectories which different communities then follow – whether benign or adverse – potentially much more destabilising.

References

Acemoglu, D. (2001) 'Technical Change, Inequality, and the Labor Market', *Journal of Economic Literature*, vol 40, no 1, pp 7-72.

Acemoglu, D. (2002) 'Cross-Country Inequality Trends', *Economic Journal*, vol 113, pp 121-49.

Adams, J. (1999) 'The social implications of hypermobility', in OECD (ed), *The economic and social implications of sustainable transportation*, Paris: OECD, pp 95-134.

Aghion, P. and Howitt, P. (1998) *Endogenous Growth Theory*, Cambridge, MA: MIT Press.

Akerblom, M. (2001) 'Constructing Internationally Comparable Indicators on the Mobility of Highly Qualified Workers: A Feasibility Study', *Science, Technology Industry Review*, No 27, Paris: OECD.

Amin, A. (1994) 'Post-Fordism: Models, Fantasies and Phantoms of Transition', in A. Amin (ed), *Post-Fordism*, Oxford: Blackwell.

Argyris, C. and Schon, D. (1996) *Organizational Learning II: Theory Method and Practice*, Reading, MA: Addison-Wesley.

Arrow, K.J. (1962) 'The Economic Implications of Learning-by-Doing', *Review of Economic Studies*, vol 29, no 1, pp 155-73.

Arrowsmith, J., Sissons, K. and Marginson, P. (2004) 'What Can "Benchmarking" offer the Open Method of Coordination?' *Journal of European Public Policy*, vol 11, no 2, pp 311-28.

Atkinson, A.B., Cantillon, B., Marlier, E. and Nolan, B. (2002) *Social Indicators: the EU and Social Inclusion*, Oxford: Oxford University Press.

Attwell, G. (2003) *E-learning and Small and Medium Enterprises*, Thessaloniki: CEDEFOP.

Ball, P. (2004) *Critical Mass: How One Thing Leads to Another*, London: Heinemann.

Barbier, C., De la Porte, C. et al (2001) 'Digest: Employment and Social Policy', *Journal of European Social Policy*, vol 11, no 1, pp 67-77.

Barro, R. and Martin, S.I. (2004) *Economic Growth*, Cambridge, MA: MIT Press.

Beccheti, Panizza, et al (2003) *Trade Performance and Industry-Specific Externalities in Industrial Districts: Evidence for the Population of Italian Firms*, Rome: ISTAT.

BEEP (2002) *Best eEurope Practices Report 4.1: report on case coding and updating*, Bologna: Nomisma.

Bell, D. (1974) *The Coming of Post-Industrial Society*, London: Heinemann.

Bennett, C. (1991) 'How States Utilise Foreign Evidence', *Journal of Public Policy*, vol 33, no 4, pp 31-54.

Bernstein, B. (1977) 'Social Class, Language and Socialisation', in J. Karabel and A.H. Halsey (ed), *Power and Ideology in Education*, Oxford: Oxford University Press, pp 473-86.

Bevan, P. (2004) 'The Dynamics of Africa's Insecurity Regimes', in I.R. Gough and G.D. Wood (ed), *Insecurity and Welfare Regimes in Asia, Africa and Latin America*, Cambridge: Cambridge University Press.

BISER (2003) *E-Business Survey 2003*, Bonn: Empirica.

BISER (2004a) *Business Enterprise in the Information Society – the Regional Dimension*, Bonn: Empirica.

BISER (2004b) *Domain Report no 10: ICT Infrastructure*, Bonn: Empirica.

BISER (2004c) *Healthcare in the Information Society – the Regional Dimension*, Bonn: Empirica.

BISER (2004d) *ICT Infrastructure – the Regional Dimension*, Bonn: Empirica.

BISER (2004e) *Work in the Information Society – the Regional Dimension*, Bonn: Empirica.

Bocconi University (2004) *Policy Recommendation Paper*, Final Report for NESIS Project.

Borghans, L. and ter Weel, B. (2001) 'How computerization changes the UK labour market: The facts viewed from a new perspective', *SKOPE Research Paper*.

Borras, S. and Jacobsson, K. (2004) 'The Open Method of Coordination and New Governance Patterns in the EU', *Journal of European Public Policy*, vol 11, no 2, pp 185-208.

Bourdieu, P. (1977) 'Cultural Reproduction and Social Reproduction', in J. Karabel and A.H. Halsey (ed), *Power and Ideology in Education*, Oxford: Oxford University Press, pp 487-510.

Bowles, S. and Gintis, H. (1976) *Schooling in Capitalist America*, London: Routledge and Kegan Paul.

Braverman, H. (1974) *Labor and monopoly capital*, New York: Monthly Review Press.

Breedveld, K. and van den Broek, A. (eds) (2001) *Trends in de tijd, een schets van recente ontwikkelingen in tijdsbesteding en tijdsordening*, den Haag: SCP

Brown, P., Green, A. and Lauder, H. (2001) *High Skills: Globalisation, Competitiveness and Skill Formation*, Oxford: Oxford University Press.

Bruce, C.S. (1999) 'Workplace experiences of information literacy', *International Journal of Information Management*, vol 19, no 1, pp 33-47.

Brynjolfsson, E. and Hitt, L. (1996) 'Paradox lost? Firm-level evidence on the returns to information systems', *Management Science*, vol 42, no 4, pp 541-58.

Buderi, R. (2000) 'Funding Central Research', *Research-Technology Management*, vol 43, no 4, pp 18-25.

Bush, V. (1945) *Science, The Endless Frontier*, Washington DC: Office of Scientific Research and Development.

Byrne, D. (1998) *Complexity Theory and the Social Sciences,* London: Routledge.

Castells, M. (2001) *The Internet galaxy, reflections on the Internet, business and society*, Oxford: Oxford University Press.

Castells, M. (ed) (2004) *The Network Society: A Cross-Cultural Perspective*, Cheltenham: Edward Elgar.

Cecchini, P. (1988) *The European Challenge: 1992: The Benefits of a Single Market*, Aldershot: Wildwood House.

CEDEFOP (2002a) *E-Learning and Training in Europe*, Thessaloniki: CEDEFOP.

CEDEFOP (2002b) *Users' Views on E-Learning*, Thessaloniki: CEDEFOP.

Checkland, P. and Scholes, J. (1990) *Soft Systems Methodology in Action*, Chichester: John Wiley.

Clayton, T. (2004a) *Globalisation and Innovation*, NESIS IDWG 3, Athens: Informer SA.

Clayton, T. (2004b) 'Serving the National Policy Users' Needs for Statistical Information on the New Economy', in D Ramprakash (ed), *NESIS Summative Conference Vol 1*, Athens: Informer SA.

Cohill, A. and Kavanaugh, A. (1997) *Community networks: lessons from Blacksburg, Virginia*, Norwood, MA: Artech House Publishers.

Cole, J. (ed) (2003) *Surveying the Digital Future, year 3*, Los Angeles, CA: UCLA Center for Communication Policy.

Cooke, P. (2004) *Regional Innovation Systems*, London: Routledge.

Cornford, J. and Pollock, N. (2003) *Putting the University on Line: Information, Technology and Organizational change*, Buckingham: Open University Press.

Coulombe, S., Tremblay, J-F. and Marchand, S. (2004) *Literacy Scores, Human Capital and Growth across Fourteen OECD Countries*, Ottawa: Statistics Canada.

Coyle, R. (1996) *Systems Dynamics Modelling: A Practical Approach*, London: Chapman and Hall.

Criscuola, C., Haskel, J. and Slaughter, M. (2004) *Why are Some Firms More Innovative?*, London: ONS.

Crouch, C., Finegold, D. and Sako, M. (1999) *Are Skills the Answer? The Political Economy of Skill Creation in Advanced Industrial Countries*, Oxford: Oxford University Press.

Currie, J. and Newson, J. (eds) (1998) *Universities and Globalization*, London: Sage Publications.

Dahlberg, L. (2002) 'Democratic Visions, Commercial Realities?', *Antepodium*, no 2 (http://www.vuw.ac.nz/atp/articles/Dahlberg_0204.html/)

Dasgupta, B. (1998) *Structural Adjustment, Global Trade and the New Political Economy of Development*, London: Zed Books.

Davenport, T.H. (2000) *Mission Critical: realizing the promise of enterprise systems*, Boston, MA: Harvard Business School Press.

David, P. (1990) 'The Dynamo and the Computer: An Historical Perspective on the Modern Productivity Paradox', *American Economic Review*. vol 80, pp 355-61.

De Haan, J. and Steyaert, J. (eds) (2003) *Jaarboek ict en Samenleving*, Amsterdam: Boom.

De Haan, M. (2003) 'Catching the Knowledge-based Economy in National Accounting', *Paper presented for the NESIS workshop on Enterprise Knowledge*, 16-17 January, Luxembourg.

De Haan, M. (2004) 'National Accounting in Post-Industrialised Economies: A Review of Possible Changes in the System of National Accounts', in D Ramprakash (ed), *NESIS Summative Conference Volume 1*, Athens: Informer SA.

De la Porte, C. and Pochet, P. (eds) (2002) *Building Social Europe through the Open Method of Coordination*, Brussels: Presses Inter-universitaires Europeennes.

De la Porte, C., Pochet, P. and Room, G. (2001) 'Social Benchmarking, Policy-Making and New Governance in the EU', *Journal of European Social Policy*, vol 11, no 1, pp 291-307.

De Panizza, A. and Fazio, A. (2004) *ISTAT – EU Qualify Pilot Study* (NESIS deliverable 5.2.1), Rome: ISTAT.

De Panizza, A., Fazio, A. and Visaggio, M. (2004) *Final Report on Review and Study of Productivity and Competitiveness Indicators: NESIS Work Package 5.2*, Rome: ISTAT.

Dedrick, J., Gurbaxani, V. and Kraemer, K. (2003) 'IT and Economic Performance: A Critical Review of the Empirical Evidence', *ACM Computing Surveys*, vol 35, no 1, pp 1-28.

Dencik, J. (2004) *Human Investment and the New Economy in the European Union*, PhD Thesis, University of Bath.

di Martino, V. (2001) *The High Road to Teleworking*, Geneva: ILO.

DiMaggio, et al (2004) 'Digital Inequality: From Unequal Access to Differentiated Use', in K. Neckerman (ed), *Social Inequality*, New York: Russell Sage Foundation, pp 355-400.

Dolowitz, D. and March, D. (1996) 'Who Learns What from Whom: A Review of the Policy Transfer Literature', *Political Studies*, vol 44, pp 343-57.

Dosi, G. and Malerba, F. (1996) 'Organisational Learning and Institutional Embeddedness', in G. Dosi and F. Malerba (ed), *Organisation and Strategy in the Evolution of the Enterprise*, Basingtoke: Macmillan.

Dunning, J.H. (1993a) *The Globalization of Business*, London: Routledge.

Dunning, J.H. (1993b) *Multinational Enterprises and the Global Economy*, Wokingham: Addison-Wesley.

ECB (2003) *New Technologies and Productivity Growth in the Euro Area*, Working Paper 122, Frankfurt: European Central Bank.

EITO (2004) *European Information Technology Observatory 2004*, Frankfurt: EITO.

ELIG (eLearning Industry Group) (undated), *Developing eLearning Communities in the EU*, Brussels: European Commission: www.elig.org

Esping-Andersen, G. (1990) *The Three Worlds of Welfare Capitalism*, Cambridge: Polity Press.

Esping-Andersen, G. (1999) *Social Foundations of Postindustrial Economies*, Oxford: Oxford University Press.

Esping-Andersen, G. et al (2002) *Why We Need a New Welfare State*, Brussels: European Commission.

Estevez-Abe, M., Iversen, T. and Soskice, D. (2001) 'Social Protection and the Formation of Skills', in P. Hall and D. Soskice (ed), *Varieties of Capitalism*, Oxford: Oxford University Press.

European Commission (1994) *Europe and the global information society (Bangemann report)*, Brussels: European Commission.

European Commission (2000a) *European Competitiveness Report 2000*, Brussels: European Commission.

European Commission (2000b) *A Memorandum on Lifelong Learning: Commission Staff Working Paper*, SEC(2000)1832, Brussels: European Commission.

European Commission (2000c) *Structural Performance Indicators*, ECFIN/330/00, Brussels: European Commission.

European Commission (2000d) *Towards a European Research Area*, European Commission.

European Commission (2001a) *Communication on an Open Method of Coordination for the Community Immigration Policy*, COM(2001) 387 final, 11.07.2001, Brussels:

European Commission (2001b) *Communication: eEurope: Impact and Priorities*, COM(2001)140), Brussels: European Commission.

European Commission (2001c) *E-inclusion, the information society's potential for social inclusion in Europe SEC (2001) 1428*, Brussels: European Commission.

European Commission (2001d) *The eLearning Action Plan: Designing Tomorrow's Education*, COM(2001)172, Brussels: European Commission.

European Commission (2001e) *Lifelong Learning Practice and Indicators*, SEC(2001)1939, Brussels: European Commission.

European Commission (2001f) *Supporting National Strategies for Safe and Sustainable Pensions through an Integrated Approach*, COM(2001) 362, 03.07.2001, Brussels: European Commission.

European Commission (2001g) *Work Programme for the Follow-Up of the Report on the Concrete Objectives of Education and Training Systems*, COM(2001)501 final, Brussels: European Commission.

European Commission (2002a) *2002 European Innovation Scoreboard: Technical Paper No 5: Lifelong Learning for Innovation*, Brussels: European Commission.

European Commission (2002b) *Commission Staff Working Paper: 2002 European Innovation Scoreboard*, SEC(2002)1349, Brussels: European Commission.

European Commission (2002c) *Communication: Action Plan for Skills and Mobility*, COM(2002)72, Brussels: European Commission.

European Commission (2002d) *Communication: Corporate Social Responsibility*, COM(2002)347 final, Brussels: European Commission.

European Commission (2002e) *Communication: eEurope 2005: Benchmarking Indicators*, COM(2002)655 final, Brussels: European Commission.

European Commission (2002f) *E-Business and ICT Skills in Europe: Benchmarking Member State Policy Initiatives*, 18.12.2002, Brussels: European Commission.

European Commission (2002g) *E-Business and ICT Skills in Europe: Synthesis Report,* Brussels.

European Commission (2002h) *eLearning: Designing Tomorrow's Education: Interim Report*, Commission Staff Working Paper, Brussels: European Commission.

European Commission (2002i) *Industrial Policy in an Enlarged Europe*, Brussels: European Commission.

European Commission (2002j) *Towards a European Research Area: Science, Technology and Innovation: Key Figures 2002*, Brussels: European Commission.

European Commission (2003a) *2003 European Innovation Scoreboard: Technical Paper No 5: National Innovation System Indicators*, Brussels: European Commission.

European Commission (2003b) *Building the Knowledge Society: Social and Human Capital Interactions*, SEC(2003)652, 28.5.2003, Brussels: European Commission.

European Commission (2003c) *Communication: Innovation Policy: Updating the Union's approach in the context of the Lisbon Strategy*, COM(2003)112 final, Brussels: European Commission.

European Commission (2003d) *Communication: Scoreboard on Implementing the Social Policy Agenda*, COM(2003)57 final, 6.2.2003, Brussels: European Commission.

European Commission (2003e) *Communication: Structural Indicators*, COM(2003)585 final, Brussels: European Commission.

European Commission (2003f) *eLearning: Designing Tomorrow's Education: A Mid-Term Report*, SEC(2003)905, Brussels: European Commission.

European Commission (2003g) *Electronic Communications: the Road to the Knowledge Economy*, Brussels: European Commission.

European Commission (2003h) *European Innovation Scoreboard 2003: Technical Paper No 1: Indicators and Definitions*, Brussels: DG Enterprise.

European Commission (2003i) *Implementing Life Long Learning Strategies in Europe: Progress Report on the Follow-Up to the Council Resolution of 2002*, Brussels: European Commission.

European Commission (2003j) *The Role of the Universities in the Europe of Knowledge*, COM(2003)0058, Brussels: European Commission.

European Commission (2003k) *Statistics on the Information Society in Europe*, Luxembourg: Eurostat.

European Commission (2004a) *Communication: The New Generation of Community Education and Training Programmes after 2006*, COM(2004) 156 final, 9.3.2004, Brussels: European Commission.

European Commission (2004b) *European Competitiveness Report 2004*, SEC(2004)1397, Brussels: European Commission.

European Commission (2004c) *Facing the Challenge: The Lisbon Strategy for Growth and Employment: Report of the High Level Group chaired by Wim Kok*, Brussels: European Commission.

European Commission (2004d) *The Financing of Higher Education in Europe*, Brussels: European Commission.

European Commission (2004e) *Innovation in Europe*, Brussels: European Commission.

European Commission (2004f) *New Indicators on Education and Training*, SEC(2004)1524, Brussels: European Commission.

European Commission (2004g) *Report on the Implementation of the Commission's Action Plan for Skills and Mobility*, COM(2004)66 final, 6.2.2004, Brussels: European Commission.

European Commission (2004h) *Social Inclusion in the New Member States: A Synthesis of the Joint Memoranda on Social Inclusion*, SEC(2004)848, Brussels: European Commission.

European Commission (2005a) *Commission Work Programme for 2005*, COM(2005)15 final, 26 Jan 2005, Brussels: European Commission.

European Commission (2005b) *Communication to the Spring European Council: Working Together for Growth and Jobs: A New Start for the Lisbon Strategy*, COM(2005)24, 2 February 2005, Brussels: European Commission.

European Commission (2005c) *eInclusion Revisited: The Local Dimension of the Information Society*, SEC(2005)206, 4.2.2005, Brussels: European Commission.

European Commission (2005d) *On-Line Availability of Public Services: How is Europe Progressing?*, Brussels: DG Information and Media.

European Commission (2005e) *Strategic Objectives 2005-2009: Europe 2010: A Partnership for European Renewal: Prosperity, Solidarity and Security*, COM(2005) 12 final, 26 Jan 2005, Brussels: European Commission.

European Commission DG Employment (2001) *The European Social Agenda and the EU's International Partners*, Conference 20-21 November, Brussels.

European Commission DG Employment (2005) *Promoting Social Development for All: the EU experience of fostering employment and social cohesion as a contribution to the Copenhagen +10 review*, Conference January 13-14, Brussels.

European Council (2000a) *eEurope Benchmarking Indicators*, 20.11.2000, Brussels: European Council.

European Council (2000b) *Lisbon European Council, Presidency Conclusions*, 23-24 March 2000, Lisbon: European Council.

European Council (2001) *Council Resolution of 8th October 2001 on e-Inclusion: Exploiting the opportunities of the information society for social inclusion (2001/C292/02)*, Brussels.

European Council (2002) *Joint Report by the Commission and the Council on Social Inclusion*, Brussels: European Council.

European Council (2003) *Towards an Inclusive Information Society in Europe*, Brussels: European Council.

European Council (2004) *Joint Report by the Commission and the Council on Social Inclusion*, 7101/04, 5 March, Brussels: European Council.

European Council and European Commission (2000) *Action Plan, eEurope: An Information Society for All*, 14.6.2000, Brussels: European Council.

European Foundation for the Improvement of Living and Working Conditions (2001) *Third European Survey on Working Conditions 2000*, Luxembourg: European Commission.

European Round Table of Industrialists (2001) *Actions for Competitiveness through the Knowledge Economy of Europe*, Report to Stockholm European Council, Brussels: European Round Table of Industrialists.

Eustace, C. (2004a) 'Measuring the Intangible Economy', in D. Ramprakash (ed), *NESIS Summative Conference Proceedings Vol 2*, Athens: Informer SA.

Eustace, C. (2004b) 'New Economy Indicators – an Intangibles Perspective', *NESIS Indicator Development Working Group*, May 2004, Athens.

Evans, M. and Davies, J. (1999) 'Understanding Policy Transfer: A Multi-Level, Multi-Disciplinary Perspective', *Public Administration*, vol 77, no 2, 361-83.

Fajertag, G. and Pochet, P. (eds) (2000) *Social Pacts in Europe – New Dynamics*, Brussels: ETUI/OSE.

Fantasia, A. (2000) 'Decoding ASPs', *Harvard Business Review*, vol 76, no 6, pp 33.

Farrell, D. (2003) 'The Real New Economy', *Harvard Business Review*, vol 81, no 10, pp 104-13.

Ferrera, M., Hemerick, A. and Rhodes, M. (2000) *The Future of the European Welfare States*, Report for the Portuguese Presidency of the European Union, Lisbon: European Council.

Fischer, C. (1992) *America calling, a social history of the telephone to 1940*, Berkeley: University of California Press.

FISTERA (2004) *(Foresight on Information Society Technologies in the European Research Area): Overview of Selected European IST Scenario Reports*, Institute for Prospective Technological Studies: http://fistera.jrc.es

Florida, R. (2002) *The Rise of the Creative Class*, New York: Basic Books.

Florida, R. and Tinagli, I. (2004) *Europe in the creative age*, London: Demos.

Forster, M. (2000) *Trends and Driving Factors in Income Distribution and Poverty in the OECD Area*, Paris: OECD.

Franzen, A. (2000), 'Does the Internet make us lonely?' *European Sociological Review*, vol 16, pp 427-38.

Galbraith, J.K. (1967) *The New Industrial State*, Harmondsworth: Penguin.

Garrett, R. (2004) *The Global Education Index 2004: Part 2: Public Companies – Relationships with Non-Profit Higher Education*, Observatory on Borderless Higher Education: www.obhe. ac.uk

Garrett, R. and Maclean, D. (2004) *The Global Education Index 2004 Part 1: Public Companies – Share Price and Financial Results*, Observatory on Borderless Higher Education: www.obhe.ac.uk

Garrett, R. and Verbik, L. (2003) *Transnational Higher Education Part 2: Shifting Markets and Emerging Trends*, Observatory on Borderless Higher Education: www.obhe.ac.uk

Gerth, H.H. and Mills, C.W. (1948) *From Max Weber: Essays in Sociology*, London: Routledge.

Giddens, A. (1990) *The Consequences of Modernity*, Cambridge: Polity Press.

Glaser, E.M., Abelson, H.H. and Garrison, K.N. (1983) *Putting knowledge to use: Facilitating the diffusion of knowledge and the implementation of planned change*, San Francisco: Jossey-Bass.

Goldthorpe, J.H. (2000) *On Sociology*, Oxford: Oxford University Press.

Goldthorpe, J.H. (2001) *Globalisation and Social Class*, Mannheim: Mannheimer Zentrum für Europäische Sozialforschung.

Goodin, R.E. et al (1999) *The Real Worlds of Welfare Capitalism*, Cambridge: Cambridge University Press.

Graham, S. and Marvin, S. (1994) 'Cherry picking and social dumping: British utilities in the 1990s', *Utilities policy*, vol 4 no 2, pp 113-19.

Granovetter, M. (1973) 'The Strength of Weak Ties', *American Journal of Sociology*, vol 78, 1360-80.

Granovetter, M. (1985) 'Economic Action and Social Structure: A Theory of Embeddedness', *American Journal of Sociology*, vol 19, pp 481-510.

Grimes, S. (2003) 'The digital economy challenge facing peripheral rural areas', *Progress in Human Geography*, vol 27, no 2, pp 174-93.

Hadjimanolis, A. (2000) 'A Resource-based View of Innovativeness in Small Firms', *Technology Analysis & Strategic Management*, vol 12, no 2, pp 263-81.

Hagmann, C. and Mccahon, C. (1993) 'Strategic Information-Systems and Competitiveness – Are Firms Ready for a IST-Driven Competitive Challenge?' *Information & Management*, vol 25, no 4, pp 183-92.

Hakim, C. (1982) 'Secondary analysis and the relationship between official and academic social research', *Sociology*, vol 16, no 1, pp 12-28.

Hall, P.A. and Soskice, D. (eds) (2001) *Varieties of Capitalism: the Institutional Foundations of Comparative Advantage*, Oxford: Oxford University Press.

Handy, C. (1989) *The Age of Unreason*, London: Business Books.

Hardey, M. (1999) 'Doctor in the house: the internet as a source of lay health knowledge and the challenge to expertise', *Sociology of Health and Illness*, vol 21, no 6, pp 820-35.

Harris, R.G. (1998) 'The Internet as a GPT: Factor Market Implications,' in E Heldman (ed), *General Purpose Technologies and Economic Growth*, Cambridge, MA: MIT.

Hart, R., Holmes, P. and Reid, J. (2001) *The Economic Impact of Patentability of Computer Programs*, Brussels: European Commission.

Hay, M. and Kamshad, K. (1994) 'Small Firm Growth: Intentions, Implementation and Impediments', *Business Strategy Review*, vol 5, no 3, pp 49-68.

HEFCE (Higher Education Funding Council for England) (2000) *The Business of Borderless Education*, London: HMSO.

Held, D. et al (1999) *Global Transformations*, Cambridge: Polity Press.

Helpman, E. and Trajtenberg, M. (1994) *A Time to Sow and a Time to Reap: Growth Based on General Purpose Technologies*, Working Paper no. 1080, London: Centre for Economic Policy Research.

High Level Group of Experts (1996) *Building the European information society for us all: first reflections of the high level group of experts*, Brussels: European Commission.

Hill, M. and Zander, K. (2001) 'DataMap: a dashboard to guide the executive team', *New Definition*, vol 16, no 1.

Hill, P. (2004) 'Satellite Accounts to Measure the New Economy', in D. Ramprakash (ed), *NESIS Summative Conference Proceedings Vol 1*, Athens: Informer SA.

Humphrey, J. et al (2003) *The Reality of E-Commerce with Developing Countries*, London School of Economics/Institute of Development Studies.

IAOS [International Association of Official Statisticians] (2002) *Conference: Official Statistics and the New Economy*, London.

ISTAT (2004) *Productivity and Competitiveness Indicators: Report on Guidelines*, NESIS Deliverable D5.3.2, Rome.

ITU (2003) *World Telecommunication Development Report 2003*, Geneva: International Telecommunication Union.

Jessop, B. (1991) *Fordism and Post-Fordism*, Lancaster: Lancaster University Working Paper.

Jones, C. (2002) *Introduction to Economic Growth*, New York: Norton.

Jorgensen, D. (2001) 'Information Technology and the New Economy', *American Economic Review*, vol 91, pp 1-32.

Jorgensen, D. (2003a) 'Information Technology and the G7 Economies', *World Economics*, vol 4, no 4, pp 139-69.

Jorgensen, D. (2003b) 'Lessons for Europe from the US Growth Resurgence', *CESifo*.

Kaiser, R. and Prange, H. (2004) 'Managing Diversity in a System of Multi-Level Governance: the Open Method of Coordination in Innovation Policy', *Journal of European Public Policy*, vol 11, no 2, pp 249-66.

Kaldor, N. (1957) 'A Model of Economic Growth', *Economic Journal*, vol 57, pp 591-624.

Kaldor, N. (1985) *Economics without Equilibrium*, Cardiff: University College Cardiff Press.

Katz, J. and Aspden, P. (1997) 'A Nation of Strangers?' *Communications of the ACM*, vol 40, no 12, pp 81-6.

Katz, J. and Rice, R. (2002) *Social Consequences of Internet Use: Access, Involvement and Interaction*, Cambridge, MA: MIT Press.

Keasey, K. and Watson, R. (1994) 'The Bank Financing Of Small Firms In UK – Issues And Evidence', *Small Business Economics*, vol 6, no 5, pp 349-62.

Kelly, K. (1997) 'New Rules for the New Economy: Twelve Dependable Principles for Thriving in a Turbulent World', *Wired*, (5.09).

Kelly, K. (1999) *New Rules for the New Economy*, London: Fourth Estate.

Kerr, C. (1964) *Industrialism and Industrial Man*, London: Oxford University Press.

Kleiner, A. and Farris, E. (2002) *Internet Access in U.S. Public Schools and Classrooms: 1994-2001*, Washington: National Center for Education Statistics.

Kline, S.J. and Rosenberg, N. (1986) 'An Overview of Innovation', in R. Landau and N. Rosenberg (ed), *The Positive Sum Strategy*, Washington DC: National Academy Press.

Knight, J. (2003) *GATS, Trade and Higher Education*, Observatory on Borderless Higher Education: www.obhe.ac.uk

Konijn, P., Moch, D. and Dalen, J. (2002) 'Searching for the European Hedonic Function for PCs', *Paper presented to IAOS Conference*, August, London.

Kraut, R. et al (2002) 'Internet Paradox Revisited', *Journal of Social Issues*, vol 58, no 1, pp 49-74.

Kraut, R. et al (1998) 'Internet paradox: A social technology that reduces social involvement and well-being?' *American Psychologist*, vol 53, no 9, pp 1017-31.

Kristensen, P.H. and Zeitlin, J. (2005) *Local Players in Global Games*, Oxford: Oxford University Press.

Krugman, P. (1991) *Geography and Trade*, Cambridge, MA: MIT Press.

Kumar, K. (1995) *From Post-Industrial to Post-Modern Society*, Oxford: Blackwell.

Larsen, K., Morris, R. and Martin, J. (2001) *Trade in Educational Services: Trends and Emerging Issues,* Paris: OECD.

Lawrence, F. (2004) *Not on the Label*, Harmondsworth: Penguin.

Lebessis, N. and Paterson, J. (2001) 'Developing New Modes of Governance', in O. De Schutter, N. Lebessis and J. Paterson (ed), *Governance in the European Union*, Luxembourg.

Lehtoranta, O. (2004) *Enterprise dynamics in the new information economy: Final report of NESIS work package 5.5*, Helsinki: Statistics Finland.

Leisering, L. and Walker, R. (eds) (1998) *The Dynamics of Modern Society*, Bristol: The Policy Press.

Levy, D. (2003) *Expanding Higher Education Capacity through Private Growth*, Observatory on Borderless Higher Education: www.obhe.ac.uk

Lipsey, R. and Bekar, C. (eds) (1995) *A Structuralist View of Technical Change and Economic Growth*, Technology, Information and Public Policy, Kingston, Ontario: John Deutsch Institute for the Study of Economic Policy.

Longstreth, F.H. and Papadopoulos, T. (2005) 'Bringing Society Back In: Theoretical and Empirical Challenges of the Second Great Transformation Thesis', paper presented to the Tenth International Karl Polanyi Conference, Istanbul, 13-16 October.

Lopez-Bassols, V. (2002) *ICT Skills and Employment*, Paris: OECD.

Lucas, R.E. (1988) 'On the Mechanics of Economic Development', *Journal of Monetary Economics*, vol 22, no 1, pp 3-42.

Lundvall, B.-A. and Tomlinson, M. (2002) 'International Benchmarking as a Policy Learning Tool', in M.J. Rodrigues (ed), *The New Knowledge Economy in Europe*, Cheltenham: Edward Elgar.

March, J. (1994) *A Primer on Decision-Making*, New York: Free Press.

Markusen, A. (1999) 'Sticky places in slippery place: a typology of industrial districts', in T. Barnes and M. Gertler (ed), *The new industrial geography*, London: Routledge: 98-123.

Marshall, A. (1920) *Principles of Economics*, London: Macmillan.

Marshall, A (1925) 'The Future of the Working Classes', in A.C. Pigou (ed), *Memorials of Alfred Marshall*, London: Macmillan.

Marshall, T.H. (1950) *Citizenship and Social Class*, Cambridge: Cambridge University Press.

Marvin, C. (1989) *When old technologies were new: thinking about electric communication in the late nineteenth century*, New York: Oxford University Press.

Massini, S. and Pettigrew, A. (2003) 'Complementarities in Organizational Innovation and Performance: Evidence from the INNFORM Survey', in A. Pettigrew et al (ed), *Innovative Forms of Organizing*, London: Sage.

May, C. (2000) *A Global Political Economy of Intellectual Property Rights*, London: Routledge.

Meijers, H. (2003) *Using ICT to measure ICT Use: Facts and Fictions*, World Summit on the Information Society, Geneva: ITU.

Menon Network (2003) *DELOS (Developing a European e-Learning Observation System) Integrated Shortlist of Indicators*, Thessaloniki: CEDEFOP.

Mercer, D. (2004) *Broadcasters Beware: Broadband Is Stealing Your Viewers*, London: Strategy Analytics.

Metcalfe, R. (1995) *From the Ether: A Network becomes more valuable as it reaches more Users: InfoWorld Magazine*, 2 October: http://www.infoworld.com/

Middlehurst, R. and Campbell, C. (2003) *Quality Assurance and Borderless Higher Education*, Observatory on Borderless Higher Education: www.obhe.ac.uk

Milgrom, P. and Roberts, J. (1995) 'Complementarities, Momentum, and the Evolution of Modern Manufacturing', *Journal of Accounting and Economics*, vol 19, no 2/3, pp 179-208.

Minges, M. (ed) (2003) *World Telecommunication Development Report 2003, Access Indicators for the Information Society*, Geneva: ITU.

Murphy, D., Zhang, W.Y. and Perris, K. (2003) *Online Learning in Asian Open Universities: resisting 'content imperialism'?*, Observatory on Borderless Higher Education: www.obhe.ac.uk

Mutch, A. (1997) 'Information literacy: An exploration', *International Journal Of Information Management*, vol 17, no 5, pp 377-86.

Naidoo, R. and Jamieson, I.M. (2004) 'Knowledge in the Marketplace', in P Ninnes and M Hellsten (ed), *Higher Education: Critical Perspectives for Critical Times*, Amsterdam: Kluwer.

Naylor, J. and Williams, J. (1994) 'The Successful Use of IT in SMEs on Merseyside', *European Journal of Information Systems*, vol 3, no 1, pp 48-56.

Nelson, R. (2000) *The Sources of Economic Growth*, Cambridge, MA: Harvard University Press.

Nelson, R. and Phelps, E. (1966) 'Investment in Humans, Technological Diffusion, and Economic Growth', *American Economic Review*, vol 61, pp 69-75.

Nelson, R. and Winter, S. (1982) *An Evolutionary Theory of Economic Change*, Cambridge, MA: Harvard University Press.

NESIS (2002) 'Proceedings', *Statistical Information System for Good Governance within the New Economy*, Conference 10-14 June, Athens: Informer SA.

Newman, F. and Couturier, L.K. (2002) *Trading Public Good in the Higher Education Market*, Observatory on Borderless Higher Education: www.obhe.ac.uk

Nie, N. and Hillygus, S. (2002a) 'The impact of internet use on sociability: time-diary findings', *IT&SOCIETY*, vol 1, no 1, pp 1-20 & www.ITandSociety.org.

Nie, N. and Hillygus, S. (2002b) 'Where does internet time come from?: a reconnaisance', *IT&SOCIETY*, vol 1, no 2, pp 1-20 & www.ITandSociety.org.

NTO (National Training Organisation) (2001) *An Assessment of Skill Needs in Information and Communication Technology*, London: Department for Education and Skills.

Nurmela, J. and Ylitalo, M. (2003) *The Evolution of the Information Society*, Helsinki: Statfin.

Nyhan, B. et al (2003a) *Facing Up to the Learning Organisation Challenge Vol 1 Key Issues from a European Perspective*, Luxembourg: CEDEFOP.

Nyhan, B. et al (2003b) *Facing Up to the Learning Organisation Challenge Vol 2 Selected European Writings*, Luxembourg: CEDEFOP.

Nyhan, B. et al (2004) 'European Perspectives on the Learning Organisation', *Journal of European Industrial Training* vol 28, no 1, pp 67-92.

OBHE (2003a) *A New Model for Indian Universities in the 21st Century*, Observatory on Borderless Higher Education: www.obhe.ac.uk

OBHE (2003b) *Online Learning in Commonwealth Universities: Part 3: Using Data from the 2002 Observatory Survey to Benchmark Institutional Development*, Observatory on Borderless Higher Education: www.obhe.ac.uk

OBHE (2004a) *Another 'Regional Education Hub' in South East Asia: Thailand Unveils its Plans as foreign universities pour in*, Observatory on Borderless Higher Education: www.obhe.ac.uk

OBHE (2004b) *Future of the UK eUniversity*, Observatory on Borderless Higher Education: www.obhe.ac.uk

OBHE (2004c) *Germany proposes 'elite universities' to enhance competitiveness*, Observatory on Borderless Higher Education: www.obhe.ac.uk

OBHE (2004d) *Malaysia to use league tables to regulate transnational activities of foreign universities*, Observatory on Borderless Higher Education: www.obhe.ac.uk

OBHE (2004e) *New Danish Internationalisation Strategy marks the end of free education for international students*, Observatory on Borderless Higher Education: www.obhe.ac.uk

OBHE (2004f) *Private Higher Education under Fire*, Observatory on Borderless Higher Education: www.obhe.ac.uk

OBHE (2004g) *Reflections on South Africa's proposed 'Code of Conduct for Transnational Delivery of Higher Education'*, Observatory on Borderless Higher Education: www.obhe.ac.uk

OBHE (2004h) *Russia's biggest private university to launch country's first 'Distance Learning Satellite Network' – implications for transnational delivery*: www.obhe.ac.uk

O'Callaghan, R. (2004) 'Growth-nodes in a Knowledge-Based Europe: a Research Roadmap', in K. Andersen and M. Vendelo (ed), *The Past and Future of Information Systems*, Oxford: Elsevier Butterworth-Heinemann.

OECD (1995) *Canberra Manual on Measuring Human Resources in Science & Technology*, Paris: OECD.

OECD (1999) *Defining and Measuring E-Commerce: A Status Report*, Paris: OECD.

OECD (2000) *Education at a Glance*, Paris: OECD.

OECD (2001) *The New Economy: Beyond the Hype*, Paris: OECD.

OECD (2002a) *Electronic Commerce Business Impact Project Background Documents*, Paris: OECD.

OECD (2002b) *Measure of Skill from Labour Force Surveys – An Assessment*, Working Party on Science and Technology Indicators, Paris: OECD.

OECD (2002c) *Measurement of Human Resources in R&D: New Indicators from the EU R&D Exercise,* Working Party on Science and Technology Indicators, Paris: OECD.

OECD (2002d) *Measuring the Information Economy,* Paris: OECD.

OECD (2002e) *Measuring the New Economy: Key Measurement Issues in International Comparisons,* Working Party on Indicators for the Information Society, Paris: OECD.

OECD (2002f) *OECD Information Technology Outlook,* Paris: OECD.

OECD (2003a) *2003 Scoreboard of Science, Technology and Industry Indicators,* Paris: OECD.

OECD (2003b) *ICT and Economic Growth,* Paris: OECD.

OECD (2004a) *Completing the Foundation for Lifelong Learning: an OECD survey of Upper Secondary Schools,* Paris: OECD.

OECD (2004b) *Counting Immigrants and Expatriates in OECD Countries: A new perspective,* Paris: OECD.

OECD (2004c) *The Economic Impact of ICT: Measurement, Evidence and Implications,* Paris: OECD.

OECD (2004d) *Human Resources in Science and Technology in India and the International Mobility of Highly Skilled Indians,* STI Working Paper 2004/7, Paris: OECD.

OECD (2004e) *Innovation in the Knowledge Economy: Implications for Education and Learning,* Paris: OECD.

OECD (2004f) *Internationalisation and Trade in Higher Education: Opportunities and Challenges,* Paris: OECD.

OECD (2004g) *OECD Science, Technology and Industry Outlook,* Paris: OECD.

OECD (2005) *Handbook on Economic Globalisation Indicators,* Paris: OECD.

OECD and Joint Research Council (JRC) (2004) *Second Workshop on Composite Indicators of Country Performance,* Paris: OECD.

ONS, UK (2003) 'Globalisation – New Needs for Statistical Measurement' paper submitted to the UN Statistical Commission and Economic Commission for Europe Conference of European Statisticians, Geneva, 10-12 June.

Orsenigo, L. (2000) 'Innovation, Organisational Capabilities and Competitiveness in a Global Economy', in K. Rubensen and H.G. Schuetze (ed), *Transition to the Knowledge Society,* Vancouver: University of British Columbia.

Paugam, S. (1995) 'The Spiral of Precariousness', in G. Room (ed), *Beyond the Threshold: The Measurement and Analysis of Social Exclusion,* Bristol: The Policy Press.

Paugam, S. (1996) 'Poverty and Social Disqualification: A Comparative Analysis of Cumulative Disadvantage in Europe', *Journal of European Social Policy*, vol 6, no 4, pp 287-304.

Petersen, A.W. et al (2004) *ICT and e-Business Skills and Training*, Thessaloniki: CEDEFOP.

Petmesidou, M. and Mossialos, E. (eds) (2005) *Social Policy Developments in Greece*, Aldershot: Ashgate.

Pettigrew, A. and Massini, S. (2003) 'Innovative Forms of Organising: Trends in Europe, Japan and the USA in the 1990s', in A. Pettigrew et al (ed), *Innovative Forms of Organising*, London: Sage.

Pettigrew, A. et al (eds) (2003) *Innovative Forms of Organising*, London: Sage.

Pew, I. (2004) *How Americans Get in Touch With Government*: www.pewinternet.org/reports/toc.asp?Report=127

Piech, K. (ed) (2003) *Economic Policy and Growth of Central and Eastern European Countries*, London: School of Slavonic and East European Studies.

Pilat, D. (2002) 'The OECD Growth Study: Some Implications for Statistics', *IAOS Conference 'Official Statistics and the New Economy'*, August, London.

Pilos, S. (2001) Report of the Eurostat Taskforce on Measuring Life-long Learning, *Seminar: Measuring Lifelong Learning*, 25-26 June, Parma.

Porter, M. (1990) *The Competitive Advantage of Nations*, London: Macmillan.

Porter, T. (2004) *Private Authority, Technical Authority and the Globalization of Accounting Standards*, paper prepared for the Amsterdam Research Centre for Corporate Governance Regulation Inaugural Workshop, Vrije Universiteit Amsterdam, 17-18 December.

Powell, J.H. and Bradford, J.P. (1998) 'The Security-Strategy Interface: Using Qualitative Process Models to relate the Security Function to Business Dynamics', *Security Journal*, vol 10, pp 151-60.

Powell, J.H. and Bradford, J.P. (2000) 'Targeting Intelligence Gathering in a Dynamic Competitive Environment', *International Journal of Information Management*, vol 20, pp 181-95.

Powell, P.L. (1992) 'Information Technology Evaluation: Is it Different?' *Journal of the Operational Research Society*, vol 43, no 1, pp 29-42.

Press, L., Foster, W., et al (2003) 'The Internet in India and China', *The Journal of Information Technologies and International Development*, vol 1, no 1, pp 41-60.

Prieger, J.E. (2003) 'The Supply Side of the Digital Divide: Is There Equal Availability in the Broadband Internet Access Market?' *Economic Inquiry*, vol 41, no 2, pp 346-63.

PriMetrica (2003) 'Global Internet Geography Database and Report' [http://www.telegeography.com/pubs/internet/reports/ig_gbl/index.html]

Putnam, R. (2000) *Bowling Alone, the Collapse and Revival of Civic America*, New York: Simon & Schuster.

Putnam, R. and Feldstein, L. (2003) *Better Together*, New York: Simon & Schuster.

Rainie, L. (2000) *Tracking Online Life*, Washington: Pew internet and American life project.

Ramprakash, D. (2004) *NESIS IDWG Third Meeting: Agenda and Addendum*, Athens: Informer SA.

Revans, R. (1980) *Action Learning*, London: Blond and Biggs.

Rheingold, H. (1993) *The virtual community, homesteading on the electronic frontier*, Reading: William Patrick.

Ricardo, D. (1821) *Principles of Political Economy and Taxation*, London: John Murray.

Roberts, J. et al (2002) *Faculty and Staff Development in Higher Education: the Key to Using ICT Appropriately?* , Observatory on Borderless Higher Education: www.obhe.ac.uk

Rogers, E. (1996) *Diffusion of Innovations*, New York: Free Press.

Rogers, E. (2003) *Diffusion of Innovations*, New York: Simon and Schuster.

Room, G. (1999) 'Social exclusion, solidarity and the challenge of globalization', *International Journal of Social Welfare*, vol 8, no 3, pp 166-74.

Room, G. (2000) 'Globalisation, Social Policy and International Standard-Setting: the Case of Higher Education Credentials', *International Journal of Social Welfare*, vol 9, no 2, pp 103-19.

Room, G. (2002) 'Education and Welfare: Recalibrating the European Debate', *Policy Studies*, vol 23, no 1, pp 37-50.

Room, G. (2003) *Report of a Joint Workshop organised by the NESIS and BEEP Projects 28th May 2003*, Brussels: University of Bath.

Room, G. (2004) 'Multi-Tiered International Welfare Systems', in I.R. Gough et al, *Insecurity and Welfare Regimes in Asia, Africa and Latin America*, Cambridge: Cambridge University Press.

Room, G. (2005) 'Policy Benchmarking in the European Union: Indicators and Ambiguities', *Policy Studies*, vol 26, no 2, pp 117-32.

Rose, M. (1994) 'Job Satisfaction, Job Skills and Personal Skills', in R. Penn, M. Rose and J. Rubery (ed), *Skill and Occupational Change*, Oxford: Oxford University Press.

Rose, M. (2003) 'Good deal, bad deal? Job Satisfaction in Occupations', *Work, Employment, and Society*, vol 17, no 3, pp 503-30.

Rubenson, K. and Schuetze, H.G. (eds) (2000) *Transition to the Knowledge Society*, Vancouver: University of British Columbia.

Ryan, Y. (2002) *Emerging Indicators of Success and Failure in Borderless Higher Education*, Observatory on Borderless Higher Education: www.obhe.ac.uk

Salvatore, D. (2003) 'The New Economy and Growth in the G-7 Countries', *Journal of Policy Modelling*, vol 25, pp 531-40.

Schaaper, M. (2004) *An Emerging Knowledge-Based Economy in China?*, STI Working Paper 2004/4, Paris: OECD.

Sciadas, G. (2002) 'Unveiling the Digital Divide', *paper to the NESIS conference in Olympia, Greece*: pp 277-308.

Sciadis, G. (ed) (2002) *Monitoring the Digital Divide ... and Beyond*, Montreal: Orbicom.

Scott Morton, M.S. (ed) (1991) *The Corporation of the 1990s*, Oxford: Oxford University Press.

Senge, P. (1990) *The Fifth Discipline*, London: Random Century.

Sermeus, W. (2003) 'Information Technology and the Organization of Patient Care', in E. Harlow and S. Webb (ed), *Information and Communication Technologies in the Welfare Services*, London: Jessica Kingsley.

Shade, L. (2003), 'Here Comes the Dot Force!: The New Cavalry for Equity?' *Gazette*, vol 65, no 2, pp 107-20.

SIBIS (2001) *Topic Report No 4: Education*, Bonn: Empirica.

SIBIS (2003a) *Benchmarking Education in the Information Society in Europe and the US*, Bonn: Empirica.

SIBIS (2003b) *Benchmarking Work, Employment and Skills in the Information Society in Europe and the US*, Bonn: Empirica.

SIBIS (2003c) *Mathing up to the information society*, Bonn: Empirica.

SIBIS (2003d) *Measuring the Information Society in the EU, the EU Accession Countries, Switzerland and the US*, Bonn: Empirica.

Simon, H. (1957) *Administrative Behaviour*, New York: The Free Press.

Smith, H.J. and Keil, M. (2003) 'The Reluctance to Report Bad News on Troubled Software Projects: a Theoretical Model', *Information Systems Journal*, vol 13, no 1, pp 69-95.

Social Protection Committee (2001) *Report on Indicators in the Field of Poverty and Social Exclusion*, Brussels: European Commission.

Soete, L. (1999) *The New Economy: A European Perspective*, Maastricht: Maastricht Research Institute on Innovation and Technology (MERIT).

Solow, R.M. (1956) 'A Contribution to the Theory of Economic Growth', *Quarterly Journal of Economics*, vol 70, no 1, pp 65-94.

Solow, R.M. (1957) 'Technical Change and the Aggregate Production Function', *Review of Economics and Statistics*, vol 39, pp 65-94.

Solow, R.M. (1987) 'We'd better watch out', *New York Times Book Review*, 36.

Statistics Finland (2004a) *eCitizenship Final Report: NESIS Deliverable 5.7.4*, Helsinki: Statfin.

Statistics Finland (2004b) *The Measurement of Knowledge Stocks and Knowledge Flows in the New Economy*, Helsinki: Statistics Finland.

Statistics Sweden (2002) *Reflecting What is New in the Economy*, Stockholm: Statistics Sweden.

Statistics Sweden (2003) *Various Ways to Reflect What is New in the Economy*, Stockholm: Statistics Sweden.

Statistics Sweden (2004) *Further Ways of Reflecting What is New in the Economy*, Stockholm: Statistics Sweden.

Steyaert, J. (2000) *Digitale vaardigheden, geletterdheid in de informatie samenleving*, den Haag: Rathenau instituut.

Steyaert, J. (2002) *Het sociale dividend van technologie*, Eindhoven: Fontys.

Steyaert, J. (2004) 'Medicijnen voor de zilveren digitale kloof', in J. de Haan, O. Klumper and J. Steyaert (ed) *Surfende senioren, kansen en bedreigingen van ict voor ouderen*, Utrecht: Academic Press.

Steyaert, J. and Gould, N. (1999) 'Social services, social work and information management: some European perspectives', *European Journal of Social Work*, vol 2, no 2, pp 165-76.

Steyaert, J. and Gould, N. (2005) 'The Rise and Fall of the Digital Divide', in J. Graham, M. Jones and S. Hick (ed), *Digital Divide and Back: Social Welfare, Technology and the New Economy*, Toronto: University of Toronto.

Stokes, D. (1997) *Pasteur's Quadrant: Basic Science and Technological Innovation*, Brookings Institution Press.

Strassman, P. (1985) *Information Payoff*, New York: Free Press.

Swan, T.W. (1956) 'Economic Growth and Capital Accumulation', *Economic Record*, vol 32, pp 334-61.

Taylor, S. and Paton, R. (2002) *Corporate Universities*, Observatory on Borderless Higher Education: www.obhe.ac.uk

Teligen (2002) *Internet Access Costs via a Standard Telephone Line, ADSL, and Cable Modem*, Brendford: Teligen.

Togati, D. (2002) 'Key Features of the New Economy', *Paper presented to the NESIS Conference 'Statistical Information System for Good Governance within the New Economy'*, 10-14 June, Olympia.

Togati, T.D. (2004) 'On the Stability of the New Economy', in D. Ramprakash (ed), *NESIS Summative Conference Proceedings Vol 1*, Athens: Informer SA.

Torres, R. (2001) *Towards a Socially Sustainable World Economy*, Geneva: ILO.

Triplett, J. (1999) 'The Solow productivity paradox: what do computers do to productivity?' *Canadian Journal Of Economics*, vol 32, no 2, pp 309-34.

Tuijnman, A. (2002) 'Measuring the Impact of the New Economy on Education Sector Outputs', *IAOS Conference 'Official Statistics and the New Economy'*, August, London.

UK Cabinet Office (2000) *Benchmarking Electronic Service Delivery, a Report by the Central IT Unit*, London: HMSO.

United Nations (2001) *Human Development Report 2001: Making New Technologies Work for Human Development*, New York: Oxford University Press.

US Bureau of Economic Analysis (2003) 'Globalisation and Multinational Companies: What are the Questions, and how well are we doing in answering them?' *Paper submitted to the UN Statistical Commission and Economic Commission for Europe Conference of European Statisticians*, 10-12 June, Geneva.

US Department of Commerce (2000) *Digital Economy 2000*, Washington DC: US Department of Commerce.

US Department of Commerce (2002a) *Digital Economy 2002*, Washington DC: US Department of Commerce.

US Department of Commerce (2002b) *A Nation Online: How Americans are Expanding Their Use of the Internet*, Washington DC: US Department of Commerce.

US Department of Commerce (2003) *Digital Economy 2003*, Washington DC: US Department of Commerce.

Uzawa, H. (1965) 'Optimum Technical Change in an Aggregative Model of Economic Growth', *International Economic Review*, vol 6, pp 18-31.

Varian, H. (2000) 'The Law of Recombinant Growth', *The Industry Standard*.

Vedder, A. and Wachbroit, R.S. (2003) 'Reliability of information on the Internet: Some distinctions', *Ethics and Information Technology*, 5(211-215).

Venezky, R.L. and David, C. (2002) 'Quo Vadis? The Transformation of Schooling in a Networked World', *Paper for the OECD/CERI Peabody College seminar*, March 25-6, Vanderbilt University.

Vidgen, R. and Wang, X. (2004) 'Adaptive Information System Development', *Proceedings of the 9th UK Association for Information Systems Conference*, Conference 5-7 March 2004, Glasgow.

Wells, M. (2004) *Digital switch to cost millions*: *The Guardian*, April 6 2004, London: 17.

Wenger, E. (1998) *Communities of Practice Learning, Meaning and Identity*, Cambridge: Cambridge University Press.

Wilensky, H. (1975) *The Welfare State and Equality*, Berkeley: University of California Press.

Winnett, A.B., Room, G. and Gould, N. (2003) 'Quality Appraisal for the NESIS Project, University of Bath', in G. Room et al, *Final Report on Conceptualisation and Analysis of the New Information Economy*, NESIS (New Economy Statistical Information System): University of Bath.

Winnett, A.B. (2004a) 'Growth and Productivity in the New Economy', in G.J. Room et al, *Final Report on Conceptualisation and Analysis of the New Information Economy*, NESIS (New Economy Statistical Information System): University of Bath.

Winnett, A.B. (2004b) 'Stability and the New Economy', in G.J. Room et al, *Final Report on Conceptualisation and Analysis of the New Information Economy*, NESIS (New Economy Statistical Information System): University of Bath.

Winnett, A.B. (2004c) 'Techniques and Transactions in the New Economy', in G.J. Room et al, *Final Report on Conceptualisation and Analysis of the New Economy*, NESIS (New Economy Statistical System): University of Bath.

Wolfe, D.A. (2000) 'Globalisation, Information and Communication Technologies, and Local and Regional Systems of Innovation', in H. Rubenson and H.G. Schuetze (ed), *Transition to the Knowledge Society*, Vancouver: University of British Columbia.

Wolters, T. (2003a) 'Frameworks for the New Economy', *Paper presented to the NESIS Indicator Development Working Group*, Athens, April 8–9.

Wolters, T. (2003b) 'Innovation and Knowledge in the Information Society', *Paper presented to the Informer Workshop on Knowledge Management*, January, Luxembourg.

World Bank (1999) *World Development Report 1998/99: Knowledge for Development*, Washington DC: World Bank.

World Economic Forum (2004) *The Global Information Technology Report 2003-2004: Towards an Equitable Information Society*, Oxford: Oxford University Press.

Young, M.F.D. (1971) *Knowledge and Control*, London: Macmillan.

Index

NOTE: Page numbers followed by *fig* or *tab* mean that information appears only in a figure or a table. Page numbers followed by *n* mean that information is in a note.

A

accounting regulation 159
Acemoglu, D. 105
'active users' 122
Adult Literacy and Life-skills Survey (ALL) 100
'adverse incorporation' 158
age and 'digital divide' 111, 131
agglomerations 32-3, 102, 150, 164*n*
  lack of indicators 157-8
Aghion, P. 31
Amsterdam: fibre-to-the-home 125
anomie 28, 105, 126
application service providers (ASPs) 67-8
Argyris, C. 36
Asia 11, 103-4
  see also China; India
Attwell, G. 91

B

Bangemann report (1994) 108-9
BEEP case studies 73
Bekar, C. 32
Bell, Daniel 1, 36
'benchlearning' 90, 144-5
benchmarking 9, 10, 29, 135
  and globalisation 152-8
  and governance 143-50, 152-3, 160-1
  dynamic change 144-5
  'intelligent' benchmarking 144, 146-9
  political choice and alternative outcomes 145-6
  human investment and learning 80, 94-5, 97
  Lisbon process 12, 14-22, 143-50, 152-3, 160-1
  ambiguity of 21-2, 143
  Open Method of Coordination 12, 14-16, 144, 150, 160-1
  assessment of 146-8
  see also dynamism and innovation; indicators
best practice
  and benchmarking 144-5
  alternative outcomes 145-6
  ICT and learning 89-90
  and knowledge management systems 55

BISER 123, 124
Bologna process 97
borderless education markets 102-4, 105
brand loyalty in higher education 93
Brynjolfsson, E. 71-2
bureaucracy theory 36
business demography indicators 69
business information systems 54
business process packages 66-7

C

Canberra Manual 84
capacity building 149-50
case management in social welfare 119
CEDEFOP 88, 99
Centre for Education Research and Innovation (CERI) 87-8
'chain-linked' innovation models 74, 121, 137
change *see* continuous change; dynamism and innovation
China
  and new economy 11
  software standards 157
citizenship: European citizenship 148, 149
civic engagement 129, 148
Clayton, T. 104, 163-4*n*
Clinton administration 2
clusters *see* agglomerations
collective ICT resources 130, 131-2
Commonwealth 6-7
Communication on Innovation Policy 51
'communities of practice' 37, 56
community
  ICT and social cohesion 115, 117, 122, 127-8
  collective ICT resources 131-2
'complementarities' 47, 74, 106, 134
complex adaptive systems theory 70, 137
composite indicators 141
computer literacy programmes 68, 113-14
'content imperialism' 103-4
continuous change
  dynamism and evolutionary economics 34-6, 41
  and organisational learning 36